301.35
Sa5m

66227

DATE DUE			
Dec 8 69			
Apr 27 70			
Mar 7 77			
May 16 '77 P			
GAYLORD M-2		PRINTED IN U.S.A.	

Making Good Communities Better

(Revised)

By IRWIN T. SANDERS

KENTUCKY PAPERBACKS
University of Kentucky Press
Lexington, 1967

PREFACE

This Handbook Has Been Written for You

IF you are an officer or a leader of a club, society, association, or any other formal group.

IF you are aiding in any community-wide effort to reduce juvenile delinquency, promote a public health program, campaign for poultry improvement—and a score of other possible projects or activities.

IF your job is the strengthening· or administration of some institution such as the church, the school, government, or a business enterprise on a local, state, or national level.

IF you are a student of society and wish to learn more about the whys and wherefores of community life.

Each person using this handbook will have different questions in mind and will have had varied experiences in community activities. For that reason, the book contains a wide range of subject matter unified by a point of view which takes into account the recognized, established principles of sound community organization.

The basic *principles* discussed in this handbook apply to all communities, whether they are small hamlets or metropolitan centers. *Techniques*, however, will vary with the size of the locality.

The general tone of the handbook will impress you as being matter-of-fact. It has no axes to grind, no great inspiration to instill. The literature on the community is full of tracts, of documents with deep spiritual insight, and of article after article urging people to do this or do that if humanity is to survive. But we can assume that you—the reader—are already involved in an organizational or community program, or else that you have already decided to try to get one started. You have the urge to do something, but you need some guide to help you decide where to take hold, how to do a better job.

Really a Headbook, Not a Handbook

This is really a *headbook*. It tells you what to *think* about, gives you a point of view, *suggests* possible solutions to problems of community organization.

This is not strictly a *handbook*. It gives you no pat formulas to apply everywhere under every condition. Rather, it emphasizes thinking before doing, and at times advises social patience rather than social action.

Acknowledgments

This handbook was begun during the war years in Washington, particularly while I was working for a summer with the Division of Farm Population and Rural Life of the Bureau of Agricultural Economics. Dr. Douglas Ensminger and Dr. Carl Taylor contributed greatly to its conception and to the ideas contained in it. Since that time, a number of other friends, too numerous to mention here, have made valuable criticisms which have been taken into account. Particular thanks are due those who prepared the Guideposts and thus added greatly to the practical usefulness of this handbook.

August 30, 1952   IRWIN T. SANDERS, Director
                                     Bureau of Community Service
                                     University of Kentucky

CONTENTS

WHAT MAKES A GOOD COMMUNITY: FOUR TRAITS

WHY DO SOME communities leave a good impression with us when we drive through them, while other towns remain a dot on our road maps? All of us are attracted by well-kept lawns, wide streets, impressive public buildings, modern stores, and clean factories. If we look behind the scenes in a good community, we find a number of traits which result in an attractive, prosperous appearance. A listing of just four of these traits—

1. Leaders that see the whole community,
2. A collective way of solving problems,
3. A strong sense of community loyalty, and
4. A basically stable economy—

will help us considerably in understanding what makes a good community.

TRAIT

1

Leaders That See the Whole Community

ONE OF MY most inspiring experiences in visiting from town to town is to come upon persons, usually in good communities, who can see their city as a whole. They see one pattern after another, but they find that each pattern is a part of the total picture of their community. As they share their broad view with others, they lay a basis for sound planning and rich, satisfying experiences for those who participate in community activities.

In many good communities doubtless much is accomplished by various leaders who pursue policies of narrow self-interest. Their mistakes cancel out after a fashion, and their city is improved by their expenditure of energy. But in those communities which really get things done, the majority of leaders have learned that the welfare of their institution, business, or profession is tied in with the welfare of others, and that progress in one area which is made at the expense of others is not really community progress.

One small city affords an interesting, though simple, case of how this awareness of the whole community grows. Its leaders were suddenly concerned with a rapid increase in juvenile delinquency and got in touch with their state university for counsel and specific aid. Social scientists made a study, reported their findings to a newly organized community council, and stood by to render any further assistance that might be desired. Local leaders, however, were even ready to move ahead on their own and tackled one problem after another. On the first anniversary of the formation of this community council a local newspaper editorialized in words such as these: "We have been thinking of our community only in economic terms until representatives from our state university showed us that social as well as economic factors were important in the development of sound community life."

As leaders we ought not only to see the whole community but to seek it, too. For a *whole* community is also a *well* community, in which problems are increasingly being solved, in which the citizens have a strong sense of loyalty, and in which the economy is basically stable.

TRAIT

2 A Collective Way of Solving Problems

EVEN GOOD communities have problems; in fact, they appear to have more problems than apathetic towns, because they tend to recognize and face up to more. But they have worked out a collective way of tackling problems. That is why good communities continue to become better.

In one community I noted considerable civic pride, but also an awareness of a big job yet to be done. When I asked some of the local people how they tackled their problems, they replied: "A few of us get interested in something, talk it up among ourselves, and then try to figure out what leading citizens know most about the problem. We generally go to them, and they help get the ball rolling. Why, only last month the water in the creek outside of town got to smelling bad, and so we went to see Dr. Williams, and he got in touch with the State Health Board to see if they could help stop the pollution. It turns out that we're going to have to do something drastic about sewage disposal around here, and so we're having a meeting next Monday night of about twenty or thirty people to see what we had better do." And so the pattern goes, problem after problem. Someone becomes disturbed and talks to his friends; they seek out qualified leaders and then rally the support of organizations.

Many communities have gone a step farther than this informal approach and have set up welfare councils, usually affiliated with the Community Chest, to take the lead in meeting pressing social problems. Others have private or semiofficial agencies to which they can take questions of economy or city planning. In the really good communities, these organizations do not pigeonhole the problems brought to them but actively strive for the improvements of their cities.

Community councils, an important form of organizational co-operation within a community, are being widely promoted by a number of state and national groups. Such councils succeed well where leaders of local groups actually feel the need of having some way of exchanging information, or a place for talking about the whole community. Such councils are short-lived where they are established within a community simply because a few people think that every community ought to have one and so push its origin before strong informed support has developed.

Where it seeks to promote projects of its own, the council frequently surrenders its clearinghouse function because it becomes concerned with a vested interest (that is, a special problem) and cannot as easily sponsor the general view. Or where it consists of leaders representing but a minority of the people in the community, it may get things done but not actually achieve widespread participation of the people within the community. The council idea does afford, however, a pattern for working together which every community should consider. Where you find an active community council you are apt to find a growing awareness of community need and ways these needs can be met. (See Guidepost 13.)

3   *A Strong Sense of Community Loyalty*

IF WE CAN win the support for needed changes in our community by appealing to the civic pride of our neighbors, our job as leaders becomes much easier, for we do not have a fight against indifference. In any town a crisis—John Brown's house burns down or the nation is at war—produces an intense loyalty; but when the crisis passes, so does civic interest. What really counts is that often hidden, strong sense of loyalty which the routine of everyday living does not dull. Such local pride is found or developed in good communities.

Unfortunately, community loyalty sometimes suffers from conflicting interests within the town. Struggles between the members of two local churches or two local political factions, for instance, can hurt local business life and education. In the good community the citizens soft-pedal those interests which divide and identify themselves with the whole town. As leaders we can strive for this ideal by providing activities in which our neighbors can work together. The feeling of co-operation coming out of such projects goes a long way toward building a strong sense of community loyalty.

Community loyalty is strong in those towns which are democratically organized, where the people understand what is going on. They know how the support of sound community programs benefits their farming, their business, their schools, their churches, and their home life. The members of each social and economic grouping know that they can trust the other groups, and they stress community loyalty above group loyalty. The community has high morale, which is really the fitting of many loyalties into such a pattern that the community strengthens rather than weakens each of them. (See Guideposts 7, 8 and 9.) This was one of the accomplishments of the traditional New England town meeting, which even today survives in urban areas. Not long ago I attended the town meeting of Needham, Massachusetts, a town with a population of about 16,000. Obviously, not all citizens could attend any one business meeting, but they could all elect a representative from their immediate locality and tell him what they thought about many questions. The business of the town was conducted by 150 of these representatives, and the rest of the auditorium was filled with interested citizens who, although they could not vote, still wanted to listen to the discussion. Many matters, from appropriating more than one million dollars for new school buildings to refusing the police force's request for higher pay, were discussed frankly and freely. Most of these issues had been studied carefully by citizens' committees, which brought in reports answering the kinds of questions the ordinary citizen might well ask. Out of such open discussions followed by prompt, efficient action community loyalty developed.

TRAIT
4   *A Basically Stable Economy*

SOUND COMMUNITY life must be based on job opportunity, adequate pay rolls, and industry diversified enough to cushion the community from the ups and downs of business cycles. Besides these, there must be enough taxable property fairly assessed to pay for the government services demanded in every modern town. Related to the question of the economic base is the area served by the community. To the extent that people from a distance are attracted in as shoppers or as patrons of the local institutions, the economic support is broadened and serves a community interest.

The economic side of community improvement has received more attention than any other trait. Chambers of Commerce, Farm Bureaus, and other organizations spend vast sums of money in developing the industry and agriculture of their communities. But a stable economy is not the only major trait. E. L. Thorndike has found from his studies of American cities that "the goodness of life in a city is explainable only in part (about one fourth) by wealth and income."

We know now what good communities have in common to make them good.

1. Leaders that see the whole community,
2. A collective way of solving problems,
3. A strong sense of community loyalty, and
4. A basically stable economy

are among the traits which make good communities. Next, let's see how communities show differences.

HOW COMMUNITIES
SHOW DIFFERENCES:
FIVE WAYS

CALIFORNIA farmers would laugh at a newcomer from the Corn Belt who tried to set up a replica of his Midwest farm in the belief that he could use the same methods to grow the same crops that he had grown back in Iowa. "The soils and climates are different," they would tell their new neighbor.

It is just as ridiculous for us to expect that all of the methods used by successful community leaders in one part of the country would work as well in another part. Our social soils and cultural climates are also different.

Before we begin a program of civic improvement, we ought to understand the particular social traits of the people of our own community. We ought to find answers to these questions:

1. In what types of leader do our neighbors place most confidence?

2. How are the people already organized to do the things they want done? In other words, what is their social organization?

3. How important to the citizens is the social ranking they give each other?

4. What methods do they use to make individuals conform to accepted standards of thought and behavior?

5. What do the people of our community consider most important in life? Or, what are their social values?

We cannot answer these questions, of course, for every community, but we can keep our discussion down to earth by drawing heavily upon studies published by the Bureau of Agricultural Economics of the United States Department of Agriculture early in the 1940's. Trained investigators went into six widely separated areas throughout the United States and remained for at least four months to observe the contemporary culture of the people. These six studies contain interesting contrasts.

In El Cerrito, a Spanish-American village along the Pecos River in New Mexico, dwell people who preserve the folkways of centuries ago. Tourists would call their manners picturesque or quaint and would be surprised at many of the local attitudes. Underlying the customary way of life of the inhabitants, however, is the fact of economic change. After the United States acquired the Southwest, the American courts reviewed the claims to the land there. The people of El Cerrito were able to keep only 5,000 acres of the original grant of 400,000 acres. They turned then to jobs with the railroads, in the beet fields, and in the mines, but by 1920 many were without work and had used up all their cash saved from better days. All that remained to them were the small tracts of irrigated land near the village. In the 1930's the people went on relief rolls, replacing their dependence upon the stockman with a dependence upon government. Their problem now is to reconcile the old with the new in such a way that life is kept stable and satisfying.

New England tradition is preserved in Landaff, in the hill country of New Hampshire. Once the inhabitants supported themselves at home and depended little upon the outside world, but now the money economy of the nearby cities has attracted the young people away from Landaff, and the older people who remain sell milk to Boston.

Harmony, Georgia, is in the Black Belt, where the coming of the boll weevil and loss of good soil shook the farmers' faith in a one-crop system. More and more they are diversifying their agriculture, although they still look upon cotton as the chief cash crop.

The Amish of Lancaster County, Pennsylvania, for hundreds of years have maintained zealously their reputation as a peculiar but plain people. They are excellent farmers who believe that only in a rural setting can they perpetuate their unique customs and creeds. They are now divided over the extent to which they should adopt such modern conveniences as electricity, the telephone, the tractor, and the automobile. The Old Order Amish fear that too much yielding will lead to the passing away of their distinctive group.

In most things, Irwin, Iowa, in the Corn Belt, takes a middle-of-the-road position. Seldom will it be representative of any extreme, because it is 100 per cent farming and yet almost 100 per cent modern. It still retains many pioneer attitudes, but it is thoroughly a part of the American way of life.

Haskell County, Kansas, is peopled largely by descendants of early American stock. They place their faith in next year's crop of wheat.   If the crop is good, they ride high; if it is poor, many face destitution and move away.   But the brave souls remain year after year in the hope of winning out once in a while in the face of recurring uncertainties.   Life with these people is a constant gamble, and this influences their daily lives in many ways.

How rich and varied is the community life that goes to make up the United States!

Now, let's look again at each of the questions raised at the beginning of this part and find our answers with reference to the places we have just read about.

W A Y
1   *Types of Leadership Confided In*

A CRUCIAL TEST of our success as community workers is the degree to which we promote group rather than personal welfare.   We may get columns of newspaper space year in and year out, make scores of speeches, give much useful advice, and yet fail in our jobs of organization, of procuring and training representative leaders who possess the traits the people want their leaders to have.

No one is a born leader.   We cannot compile a list of leadership traits, find someone who has all these characteristics, and expect him to lead automatically wherever we may place him.   Nothing is farther from the truth than the statement that certain leadership traits hold good for all societies and for all situations within any one society.   On the contrary, each culture area must be studied in its own right to determine what type of leader the people prefer to follow. A look at the communities we have already described reveals this fact clearly.

In El Cerrito the people respect age, family background, and the ability to express oneself fluently. They like a smooth talker, because so many of them find self-expression difficult and laborious.

In Haskell County, Kansas, people are suspicious of professional leadership, even considering specialists cocky. The men try to avoid leadership, while the women seek it—and make dynamic leaders, too. In fact, the men do not want to become organizational leaders because a leader is supposed to be direct, blunt, frank. He runs the risk of antagonizing those who disagree with him. But by and large, leadership is exerted informally behind the scenes, and the real leaders among the men seldom are elected to office.

The people of Landaff, New Hampshire, have little use for the aggressive person who gets things done. The real leaders have high social standing because of their substantial farms and long residence. They are expected to carry out the duties of their office, but not to go beyond them. They must have the prime virtues of this culture: self-reliance, respect for others, and independence. They are not to introduce changes but to preserve the traditional.

We can see from these three examples that an understanding of the leadership preferences of the community in which we work will help us in these ways:

1. Once we decide what groups we want to reach, we will know better what key persons to consult first. Approaching the right people is more than half the battle of winning public support.

2. By understanding this leadership-followership aspect, we can anticipate the kind of leader which the people will choose, and so we can get to work with new officers immediately after their election instead of first having to get acquainted with their habits. Usually, we will have thought out in advance some suggestions which will start a discussion among the leaders and lead them to a satisfactory plan of action.

3. We will understand also why officers must prepare different plans of action for different social groupings within a certain culture or for situations involving two different culture areas.

W A Y
2   *Kinds of Social Organization*

WE ALREADY know that the people with whom we work have traditional ways of doing the things they think need to be done. Some activities they leave up to their school or to their church, others to their family, and still others to the government or to business. In some places the people also get things done through organized groups such as co-operatives, luncheon clubs, the Grange, Masonic orders, and the like (see Guidepost 5); in others, because they are not used to formal organizations, they prefer to work informally on a person-to-person basis.

Since in every community there is already an established way of getting particular things done, we must use as far as possible the existing setup in order to achieve the best results.

Let's take the case of El Cerrito, the Spanish-American village. In this community the church is influential even to the extent of providing the people with recreation, including serenades and horse races. The priest advises with the people in many of their personal problems and writes letters for the illiterate. There are few other formal organizations in the area except the church and the family groups. The family is a closely knit unit which teams up with the church in helping people meet the chief needs of life. Although economic factors are changing this church-family pattern, it still exists as an important traditional force to be reckoned with in the promotion of any program. As the priest said, "If the church and the outside agencies would only work together on local problems, co-operation from the people would be much easier to secure."

In contrast to El Cerrito, the people of Landaff, New Hampshire, consider the church of minor importance; in fact, probably less influential than the Grange. The family, though, in spite of its early emphasis upon personal independence, is still the basic feature of organizational life. Family groups tend to live and let live, complicating their existence as little as possible by contact with formal groups of many kinds. The town meeting periodically fulfills its political function, but it remains essentially simple in structure. Any worker who sought to apply in Landaff high-pressure salesmanship and publicity-demanding techniques would create more amusement than co-operation. His best possibility would be to work through the Grange, the annual town meeting, and perhaps even more helpfully on an informal face-to-face basis with various families whom he has reason to believe would be interested in his program. Some formal organization quite possibly could result, but certainly not before the traditional approach had created a public opinion ready to support it.

These illustrations emphasize these points of importance to us:

1. There is a traditional pattern of organization, a tendency to emphasize some local institutions or organizations at the expense of others, in every community.

2. In addition to these groupings there are many cases in which people associate frequently on an informal basis. Some of these groups are highly important in their effect upon community thinking. In fact, *informal groups run the average community.* On the surface, in the rural communities many of these seem simply loafing groups: farmers swapping yarns at the milk station, at the grain elevators, at the crossroads store, around the cotton gin, the feed store, or the garage. If the same men get together often enough in the same place, they may be regarded as a group, informal though it be. The men, however, are not the only ones who belong to informal groupings. Farm women have the party line and the habit of borrowing something from a neighbor where two or three other women may also be chatting. "I'm going visiting" is the way a woman often announces that an informal group is assembling.

3. But the informal groupings in the *village* or *town* must not be overlooked. Examples in cities are the courthouse political clique, businessmen dropping into a banker's office for a while each morning, lunching together at noon, or playing golf in the afternoon or cards on Saturday night. The affairs of the community are aired and an agreement often is reached about some

particular problem. These men through their various contacts bring others around to the point of view accepted by the informal grouping. Women, likewise, have their get-togethers at which they thresh out the way some local problem should be treated.

The approval or disapproval, therefore, of such informal groups is often a more potent force in success or failure than columns of newspaper publicity. The reason is this: *the community is already organized and these informal groups are definitely a part of that organization.*

4. Most of these well-defined groupings have their spokesmen, or people who represent their interests. Knowing who speaks for the businessmen, the landowners, and various minority groups is a big help in making contacts and organizational plans.

5. At all times we should be aware of these social patterns. Wherever possible we should fit our organizational approach into them, although we may eventually expect to end up with something new. It is like grafting a new branch to an old tree.

W A Y
3   *Importance of Social Ranking*

As COMMUNITY workers, in drawing up plans we must decide just which groups we wish to reach. To do this, we must know what groups there are. Unfortunately, many leaders do not realize that some of the most important groups have no name, no set of officers, no official meetings. These are part of the informal groups just mentioned above. The community has its labels for these divisions, such as "the four hundred," "the village people," "reliefers," "floaters," "the old families," "landowners," "tenants," and the like. The reasons why some people have a high standing and others a low standing in a community vary with the culture areas.

Where the whole population is shifting or where people want to keep everybody on the same level, the kind of person you are determines to a large degree the position you achieve. In other areas, where there are sharply divided social groupings, *who you are* is more important than *what you are*. In these latter areas your social status is determined by your sex, race, nationality, economic position, occupation, length of residence, and family background. In other words, your place may depend very little upon whether you do or do not have desirable personality characteristics; it may depend instead upon factors over which you as an individual have little control, such as parentage and family name.

A community worker, therefore, who would reach a given group of citizens must see that positions of responsibility fall upon individuals whom the others accept. Much social waste and even personal embarrassment result from pushing an unwanted leader upon those with socially inherited prejudices against that individual and the status he represents. This also works two ways: those considered socially inferior by the community often resent the advances of the socially superior just as much as, if not more than, those at the top resent the attempt of a socially inferior person to represent them in some community enterprise.

The community studies we have been using reveal

marked differences in the way people rank themselves in relation to one another. Among the Pennsylvania Amish the man is the head of the house, but there is little hereditary class structure. The variations in prestige are based upon a well-kept barn and house, good stock, and good farm machinery.

In Landaff, New Hampshire, there are considerable class differences, based primarily upon economic factors. The groups are the farm owners who run local organizations and control local government, the part-time farmers and the few tenants, the laborers who reside in the area, and the floaters who move in and out. Family descent, long residence, and an emphasis upon the traditional virtues are also important.

Harmony, Georgia, represents an area complicated by racial divisions. Not only do the whites and Negroes assume positions in relation to each other, but they are classified further within their own racial groups. Among the whites the owners, especially those from the old families with a plantation tradition, rank at the top. These whom the community considers superior resent those whom they consider the scum now coming in. This is primarily because the newcomers challenge the established position of the old families.

In Haskell County, Kansas, on the other hand, the communities are not highly stratified, although there are two sharply divided groups: the Mennonites, a minority who, like the Amish, hold themselves apart from the majority of people, who they term the "Gentiles." These latter call themselves the "whites."

In Irwin, Iowa, the earlier feeling of difference between the villager and the farmer has changed to positive co-operation, because both groups now realize that they are dependent upon the economic returns from farming. El Cerrito has little class structure, but does give the man a much higher position than the woman.

These case studies show us that in terms of selecting people to help him, a community worker in Haskell County, Irwin, and among the Amish would do best to give weight to personal characteristics, but in Harmony, Landaff, and El Cerrito he would have to place importance in inherited social and economic position. For us in our work, they show that where the society does come in fairly clearly defined layers,

1. We must choose to back our program those who are acceptable to the social layer to which we want to appeal. For example, a promising young businessman, recently settled in the community, should not be expected to represent the old established families.

2. A program seeking to enlist the aid of the whole community must be endorsed by people from each important status in the community. Merely soliciting the help of leading citizens is not enough; one needs rather the participation of *representative* citizens.

W A Y
4

Methods Used
to Make Individuals Conform

As COMMUNITY workers we are seeking constantly by foresight and careful planning to prevent anything happening which would hinder our program and to encourage whatever fosters its growth. Our ability to do this is increased greatly if we know what methods the people of our community use to make individuals conform to accepted standards of behavior.

In Harmony, Georgia, for example, the Negro church is an important means of keeping its members in line, while the white church has slight effect in that way. In Haskell County, Kansas, people resort to gossip, curiosity about their neighbors' activities, and gestures of disapproval. The Amish have developed numerous techniques to make an offender repent. These range from the weeping of women to excommunication or shunning. The person who is shunned must eat at a table apart from members of even the immediate family.

The people of Landaff, New Hampshire, seldom express any social condemnation directly to nonconforming persons. They gossip a good deal, but on the whole they value their own independence and will grant independence of action to others, saying "He pays his bills; so he can do as he likes."

The values of sizing up the social pressures in our own community are these:

1. Since almost any organizational effort will arouse some opposition, we should know what the reaction of people will be to our program. Far too often a county agent or school principal, for instance, is so afraid of meeting opposition of any sort that he plays safe—so safe that he gets little or nothing done.

2. By knowing how praise, public recognition, election to office, and so on act as positive pressures in our community, we can counteract certain opposition. In some areas praise goes a long way; in others it is confused with flattery and received suspiciously, especially from newcomers. Or again, putting one person in the limelight may make the others envious and less co-operative; in another area people would bask in the

reflected glory and think it just fine that John Smith's
good work was recognized.

3. We will realize that social control—the methods
used to make an individual conform—need not be un-
democratic and are necessary for any living together.
In a democracy, however, the effective controls are kept
in the hands of the followers, not surrendered to dicta-
torial, ambitious leaders.

W A Y
5   *Systems of Social Values*

SOCIAL VALUES are the key to understanding a community. If we know what the people in a
certain area consider the most important things in life,
we know their social values. It takes little imagination to see the relationship between their values and
their views on leaders, their status system, and their
means of social control. If people are quite well agreed
on the relative importance of various things in life, their
culture is stable; if they have widely different inter-
pretations, we may be sure that a culture is breaking
down, probably under the impact of another culture
more suited to present needs and events. On the other
hand, where social divisions are clearly drawn, two or
more systems of social values may exist side by side
for a long time.

People are going to evaluate our program in keeping
with their scale of values. If we represent something
they consider important, all the weight of tradition and
group sentiment will back us up. If our program has
little connection with what they think important, we

are in for a difficult time. Our one way of approach in that case would be to interpret our program so that it would tie in directly with the primary social values of the community.

We can illustrate this by taking three values—thrift and debt, co-operation, and education—from the six studies we have been using. In the Kansas county, penny pinching is frowned upon and debt is an expected state of affairs. Similarly in Harmony, Georgia, the planter tradition of enjoying life is still so strong that the people say, "Money is made round so that it will roll." On the other hand, the Spanish-Americans of El Cerrito are learning the importance of keeping out of debt, not because they stress thrift but because debt frequently has meant foreclosure and the loss of the home, their most cherished possession. In Iowa there is a promptness in paying one's bills and a general attitude of squeezing the orange pretty dry. It does not duplicate the thrift of Landaff, New Hampshire, which borders on miserliness prompted mainly by the desire to be independent and the difficulty of the economic struggle in the days of settlement, nor is it the thriftiness of the Amish, which by tradition is a part of their religion. It partakes of both of these, however, because pioneer attitudes that were largely Puritan are still strong. It is easy to see that a program which stressed primarily the money it would save would meet with a varied response in these six communities.

Co-operation is one of those much abused words which mean different things to different people. Some people resent being called unco-operative even though by every standard they actually are. In Landaff, New Hampshire, there is little interfamily co-operation because of the great stress placed upon individualism and pride in personal accomplishments. In Iowa, where pioneering meant neighborhood co-operation and sharing of tools and large machines, neighbors are expected as a matter of course to trade implements and to contribute their full share of work in threshing rings. Co-operation is less highly valued in Haskell County, Kansas, where successful pioneering meant large-scale farming and thus large machine farming. Among the Spanish-Americans there are times when co-operation is expected without fail: notably, when the irrigation ditch is cleaned. The Amish work together in barn-raisings and the like, but they join only those co-operative organizations where membership is informal and signatures are not required. If a program emphasizing the importance of co-operation should be tried in each of the culture areas, it would stand little chance of acceptance in Landaff and Haskell County, unless with this appeal there went some other feature that would win support.

Because the Haskell County people will do anything for their children, they support the schools wholeheartedly, often beyond the limit of their financial ability. In contrast, the Amish want the schools to teach only the three R's and no more. The parents, not the state, are held responsible for teaching children what they should learn.

Value after value would illustrate different degrees of acceptance in these varying communities. The three we have discussed are enough to show that:

1. We have a key to the understanding of our community if we understand its social values.

2. General agreement among the people on values

indicates a stable culture; general disagreement reveals an unstable or transitional culture.

3. In order to have our program accepted, we must interpret it and explain it in terms of the values of the community. If it seems necessary to run counter to these values in special cases where something quite new is proposed, we should cite examples of other communities where the change has been accepted.

4. Since in any one community there may be two or more well-established value systems which differ, we may have to evaluate our aims in terms of the specific cultural group we are trying to reach.

The above conclusions have been based on the analysis of data from six rather small rural communities. Would they hold true for larger towns and cities? Available evidence indicates that they would. First, there are the Lynds' classic work, *Middletown, A Study in Contemporary American Culture* (New York, 1929) and their follow-up description of the same Indiana community, *Middletown in Transition* (New York, 1937) which clearly set forth the social values, the reliance on social organizations, and the social rankings within this industrial city. The studies of W. Lloyd Warner and his associates in *The Yankee City Series* (New Haven, 1941-1946) reveal differences as well as similarities in the communities studied, illustrating the point that most community programs must be considered carefully in the light of the social traits of each given community. Two other studies add further evidence: James West, *Plowville, U.S.A.* (New York, 1945) and A. B. Hollingshead, *Elmtown's Youth* (New York, 1949).

Studies of much larger metropolitan areas bear out the everyday observations that here too the subcommunities attached to the metropolis differ significantly in character from each other.

As has been already indicated, there are important uniformities that run through community living, and much of this handbook will deal with these. But concentration on these similarities should not make us forget the individuality of each community and the important consideration growing out of this.

In the culture of any people there are customs ready to assist or to hinder us, depending upon how we use them. Like the woodworker, we can go with or against the grain. But first we must see the customs, we must be conscious of the grain. There are five cultured considerations, important for organization.

1. Qualities desired in leaders vary from community to community and even from activity to activity. *We must know and make use of the characteristics of leadership in our own particular area.*

2. People are organized already to do what they think needs to be done. Their organization may not be efficient, but it is there. *Wherever possible, we should use—not compete with—these established ways.*

3. Many communities have a status system. *We ought to recognize this system in getting representative helpers for our program.*

4. There are accepted ways of persuading people to co-operate in programs. *We should use these means of social control in selling our program.*

5. Social values are what the people consider most important in life. *We must be sure our program's approach is related to outstanding community values.*

We could go on talking about the characteristics of communities for many more pages, but it is time we swing into action. Let's look now at how to promote a program or project.

HOW TO PROMOTE
A CIVIC PROGRAM:
FIVE STAGES

A WARM-HEARTED club president found herself slightly at sea when she read over the suggestions I had to make in this part of the book. Her remarks showed that she had missed the point of this whole section since she did not know just what questions it was supposed to answer. Her concentration had been so wholeheartedly on her Tulip Civic Club that she had forgotten the community. Once properly briefed, she reread the material and became an enthusiastic champion of the five-stage approach in promoting a program.

The pointers I gave my friend may help other readers, too.

1. We are talking about programs for the *whole community*, not just about activities carried out by one organization for its own enrichment.

2. We are talking about those points important in all kinds of program, not about the specialized techniques most useful in a particular sort of campaign. Both a group of citizens promoting a dog-catching campaign and another a drive to provide milk for school children will find in this book how to win public support, although neither will be told what is the best

equipment for catching dogs or for refrigerating milk.

3. What we are talking about in this section will be much more meaningful if we have read carefully Parts 1 and 2.

From the time someone gets an idea to the completion of some project resulting from the idea, a program goes through five definite stages:

1. Rooting the idea,
2. Getting the facts,
3. Planning a program,
4. Launching the program, and
5. Keeping up with the program.

There is nothing sacred about the number five; frequently some of the stages move ahead rather quickly, despite the detail with which they are treated here. Nevertheless, thinking in terms of all five stages will help us be systematic. We will be able to talk about concrete steps when we are discussing our program with someone who is not yet warmed up to the subject. Many people eager to help out have turned their backs on a program simply because someone connected with it could talk only in vague generalities. On the other hand, it makes sense to hear a worker talk about his proposals knowingly: "I've an idea that the community is ready to do something about clearing out the slums, but before we get too far we ought to get the facts. Then we can plan a program in the light of those facts, launch it, and sell the community on supporting a sound course of action. Afterward we can evaluate our experience in order to make the rest of the program more effective." When they hear that kind of talk, people can decide at what point they can make their best contribution and are willing to follow the lead of someone who knows where the program is heading.

S T A G E

1   *Rooting the Idea*

MANY COMMUNITY programs start with someone who has an idea that he cannot put into effect by himself. He tells others in his club or informal group about it. They give him encouragement, and a beginning is made.

Such was the case with Art Smith, a fireman riding back on a truck from a run. The fire he had helped put out started because some oily rags had been left carelessly in the basement. He wondered why his community shouldn't have a Fire Prevention Day on which school children would be given rides in fire trucks and then sent home to look from attic to cellar for fire hazards. He talked it over with his chief. They went to the editor of the local paper to ask his opinion. He told them that the idea would go over big if they persuaded Hamilton Lawrence, Jr., the local bank president, to sponsor it and appoint the necessary committees. They do; it does.

Other community programs start because groups want to do something for their community and are on the lookout for an idea. They call for suggestions and choose projects from the many that are proposed. In such a case, the project from the beginning is group-sponsored and grows as the original group enlarges the circle of those taking part in the work.

Often it is hard to trace the beginning. Something

dramatic in community life—the arrest of a juvenile delinquent, a series of airplane crashes, a strike—may cause many persons to decide almost simultaneously upon the need for a particular line of action.

But in most cases, the idea comes from outside the community. Some long-time resident takes a trip, attends a convention, takes an out-of-town job temporarily. He sees or hears about something significant happening in another community and says to himself, "Why can't we do the same thing back home?" He asks more questions about what he has observed, so that when he goes home he is ready to do a job of community building. That is why so many veterans on their return launched into movements to improve their home towns. They had seen what other folks could do.

Or perhaps a newcomer to the community has been active in projects in the town where he used to live. Slowly but surely, as he gets the feel of his new home town and wins the confidence of his new neighbors, he suggests ways of dealing with some local problem. A newcomer may help unknowingly in another way; he may stand out like a sore thumb and by his very presence afford contrasts spurring local folks to action.

Again, a professionally trained outsider may be employed locally or else visit the community for a short time to persuade the local people to sponsor and carry through some program. City planning experts and county agricultural agents are examples of persons whose talents may be imported into a community. Clergymen and school administrators too, because they move from one community to another, are looked upon as outsiders, but are expected to suggest innovations wherever they happen to be employed at the moment.

Executives of social agencies, chamber of commerce secretaries, labor leaders—whether native or imported—are supposed to know about national trends in order to keep the community up to date. They patiently sow seeds with board members, year in and year out, and quite to their amazement occasionally see a harvest come to fruit.

An idea remains an idea, however, unless we give it root. There are several steps which we can take to do this.

1. We must first write out clearly what we have in mind, so that in talking about our idea we can keep to the point. We ought to realize, nevertheless, that our original written statement may be quite different from that prepared by the planning group once our idea has been accepted for investigation and possible action. We can often help to make our idea appear more concrete by having pictures of what other towns have done. I recall a case of a community leader who made little progress in winning interest for a highway beautification plan which called for improvement of the approaches to the town until she showed a few businessmen and other club women before-and-after pictures of what a neighboring community had done.

2. Before we push our idea far, we ought to consult experts in community organization. (See Guidepost 1.) They not only can tell us the easiest way of going about the task in our community, but also can supply us with considerable information about what other towns have done along the lines in which we are interested.

3. We must select carefully those whom we approach first. For one thing, we must choose persons who have the confidence of the majority of the community mem-

bers. We should also try to see in advance any influential persons who we think might be indifferent or opposed to our plan; many will be active supporters if they understand. If they remain hostile, we will know in the beginning what kind of opposition we face.

4. If possible, we will begin with a need the people feel. A town, for instance, that is greatly disturbed about its water supply is much more likely to go along with a program to improve it than with one calling for a public swimming pool in the park, even though everyone would agree readily that a swimming pool would be a fine thing.

Regardless of how it began or how it was rooted, an idea is on its way when enough competent people are talking it over with one another. Maybe only a few people are as yet in the know, but the idea has passed from a single champion to several who are exploring ways of getting something done. Now it is time to get the facts.

STAGE

2   *Getting the Facts*

THIS SECOND stage is the one that many workers would like to skip, and frequently do skip to their own misfortune. They become so enamored with an idea and everything seems so perfectly clear to them that they see no reason for postponing action. But there are important values in going through the fact-finding stage.

1. Facts are valuable in planning. Although they have lived a long time in a community, many people

will disagree over points which anyone could observe with little difficulty. When such differences arise, the leader ought to be able to say, "Let's look at the facts before we get involved in an argument." Facts, not "guesstimates," are most important, too, in estimating the cost of a program. In the center of a town I know of there stands an unfinished community house, a symbol of failure. A few enthusiastic persons got the idea that the town needed a community center and immediately began to raise funds. When the first money came in, they let the contract for the building and talked imaginatively of the ways they would raise the rest of the money to pay for the project. But fellow townspeople did not share their enthusiasm; the would-be community workers not only overestimated the town's ability to pay for such a building, but learned that their neighbors didn't really want a community house in the first place. Even the simplest of surveys could have predicted danger signals on both these counts.

2. Fact-finding develops teamwork. One of the best guarantees of success in promoting a program is adequate teamwork which doesn't spring up full-blown overnight. It is achieved gradually. The fact-finding stage is a splendid opportunity for a number of people to get to know each other and to compare notes on what they are finding out. Leadership skills come to light and give indications of the persons who should be asked to carry responsibilities in the later stages. Furthermore, fact-finding is a less complicated channel for developing teamwork than some of the later stages where friction and differences of opinion could enter in to discourage co-operation. With the pattern

of teamwork set early, there is a carry-over into periods of difficulty ahead.

3. Fact-finding gives an opportunity for broad participation. The more people are enlisted in a program in its early stages the greater the support for that program in the community at large. Fact-finding is one area in which many people can be asked to help, particularly if they are given specific instructions ahead of time and are not expected to cover too big an assignment. One community used sixty volunteer citizens to make a house-to-house canvass in a fact-finding survey prior to the formation of a community council. These interviewers were given four simple questions to ask and were told how to record the information obtained. The task was planned so that almost all of them felt successful at the end and all knew that they had contributed to the formation of the council. They were likely to maintain a personal interest in it during the years ahead. Such an approach overcomes the frequent criticism that a small group is trying to stir something up in the community for selfish purposes.

4. Fact-finding educates. One couple who had undertaken to aid in a survey seeking to locate boarding homes for underprivileged children returned from an afternoon's visiting with consternation written all over their faces. They had been given as a routine matter two city blocks to cover and by chance had drawn a run-down residential district. Although they both had thought that they knew their community, they quickly confessed that they never realized that people were living like those whom they visited. The woman exclaimed, "I saw a six-months-old baby being given a piece of raw bacon to suck," while the man was im-

pressed by the fact that five window panes in a kitchen were broken with no concern being expressed that they be replaced. In other words, these fact-finders were being educated in a direct way and would know where-of they spoke when they talked about certain community needs. Then, too, the *people visited* are informed about what is afoot. The interviewer has to make a brief explanation about the purpose of the survey and thus prepares the ground for the official launching later on. Oftentimes people will answer, "Why, I never thought about that question before," indicating that the educative process is getting a start.

So, in a number of ways the time and trouble involved in getting at the facts pays off royally in dividends of understanding, teamwork, and a community readiness to support the program. (See Guideposts 2, 3, 4, and 5.)

Now that we know that the fact-finding stage is necessary, we need to find out what facts to collect. These will vary, of course, with the kind and the scope of our program, but some general guides are useful.

1. *Use specialists.* We ought by all means to seek the help of fact-finding specialists, especially if we did not call in an expert during the first stage of getting the idea well rooted. This usually saves time on two counts. First, with proper advice we will know what facts will be most helpful and can eliminate the many things which would be interesting to know but which have little direct bearing on our problem. Secondly, we can be shown shortcuts in the preparation of schedules, population samplings, methods of tallying, and be warned against the misuse of statistics in our interpretation. This all sounds formidable and most diffi-

cult to a worker who is interested simply in persuading others to start an annual strawberry festival, but he would find himself making much more rapid progress if, after getting the support of a few people, he studied the types of activity people most preferred in such a festival. Rural people, too, would be reached, so that the affair would not be just town-centered but would really serve the whole community.

2. *Decide what facts are already available.* We should use whatever facts have already been collected. Many citizens feel that they are plagued with too many surveys. It often happens, however, that there is no reliable, up-to-date information about the problem being studied, and in that case we will need to have a survey. We must beware, however, of a failing common to small towns, where people say, "What's the use of the fact-finding stage when I can count on my fingers the number of churches, clubs, and agencies here." All too often an important group is accidentally overlooked.

3. *What other information is needed?* Once we have made use of the data at hand, we must decide what other information we need. The workers on our project should draw up a long list of questions which have a bearing on the problem. This list should be passed around for appraisal by business leaders, city and county officials, and others with community-wide experience. Such a step means usually the whittling down of the list somewhat, for these men with practical experience will say, "That's a fine question you have there, but you just won't get any reliable information on that. People won't give a stranger facts such as those." Other questions will be eliminated on other grounds, such as showing a bias for or against some

community faction or dealing with a technical problem beyond the grasp of most people.

4. *Test questions.* Now we ought to try out our revised list of questions on a number of people. Do they really understand the question, or is the phrasing misleading? Is it couched in their language? Is the question loaded, suggesting the answer that the one interviewed is supposed to give? This trial will show what revisions are needed both in the wording of the questions and in the way the project is explained.

5. *Always have group sponsors.* At last the schedule of questions is ready. We are ready to ask responsible local committees or organizations with high, established prestige to undertake the survey, for they are in position to solicit public support and to provide adequate financial backing. Our job is to sell these sponsors on the purpose of the survey and to convince them of its need. This will be much easier if they have already had a part in the preparation of the survey questions. I know of a wealthy man who thought it would be a splendid idea if the school children of his community all had hot lunches. He set out with a few paid helpers to learn what the parents thought of this plan. His list of questions contained rather intimate questions about diet and food budgets, and in about three cases out of five his interviewers got inadequate information. The chances are that workers representing PTA's or women's clubs would have gotten a much better response from the people who were supposed to benefit, and they probably would have drawn up a more practical schedule, too. We cannot afford to let the citizens think that the survey is an individual and not a community effort.

6. *Train interviewers.* We must train carefully those who are to do any interviewing for any major survey. We must be sure that they state the purpose of their call clearly, that they ask the questions distinctly, and that they record the answers accurately. We might suggest the best way to approach people through pleasantries about the weather, children, and the like; arranging for appointments by telephone or post card; the length of time to be given to an interview. We should tell the interviewers whether or not to record the valuable side remarks made by the informants which, although not in direct answer to the question, reveal what people think about topics related to the problem being studied. Every interviewer should be given one or two practice interviews, possibly practicing upon others who also plan to help with the survey, to be followed with a reminder of do's and don'ts.

7. *Tabulate results.* As soon as the schedules are completed, we should tabulate the results. If we have trained our interviewers well, their results should be comparable. Someone in the community with at least slight statistical experience could be asked to help in tallying the questions in a general summary.

8. *Interpret results.* Now we are ready to interpret the results, to give them meaning, but we must be careful to do this in the light of the social traits of our own community. Every careful survey will include not only data about material things, but also will give some attention to the existence of groups interested in the problem being studied, to antagonism or competition present in the community, as well as the leaders who serve as spokesman for large segments of the population. If we have included such information in our

fact-finding, we will have an easier job of interpretation.

9. *Prepare graphic reports.* Our last job in the fact-finding stage is the presentation of what we have found. We can do this most clearly by asking someone with the necessary skills to prepare charts and sketches setting forth the findings. People usually master statistical reports better through the eyes than through the ears; a chart is worth many columns of figures.

The stage of fact-finding, because of the concentration upon details, can easily be made an end in itself. People may come to believe that all they have to do is to prepare a report; the report is supposed to solve the problems. If we are alert to our jobs, we will realize that fact-finding serves only as an avenue to the next stage—planning a problem.

STAGE

3 *Planning a Program*

A MOST CRUCIAL step is from fact-finding to planning. The final success of a program depends not only upon the plan itself, but also upon the people chosen to help with the planning. We have to select a few objectives from a large number indicated by the facts we have gathered; we have to develop a strategy in the approach toward these objectives; and we have to consider what resources are at hand, how we can sell the program to the public, and how much success we can reasonably expect.

Before we go farther, let's agree on what we mean by a program. A program is a preliminary statement which gives a general plan of projected action. It is the explanation of a group's policy so that various people can find out just how the policy affects them. A good program states three things: what is to be done *(policy)*, how it is to be done *(organization)*, and why it is to be done *(motivation)*.

There are several ways to develop a program. At one extreme we have the autocratic method, in which one person, or at best a few people, take matters into their own hands and decide just how things are to be done down to the last detail. Their planning finished, they give specific orders and expect people to swing into action all the way down the line. At the other extreme we have the democratic method, in which as far as possible the people who are to be affected by the program have some part in its determination. Experience has shown over and over again that people in communities throughout the land respond more readily to the democratic than to the autocratic approach.

Another question of major importance is deciding who should take part in the early stages, who should be in on the ground floor. We should include in the planning those people who actually know the field to which the program is related. Their familiarity with actual situations helps them avoid mistakes which the less experienced would be likely to make. But here is where the out-of-town expert, if he has not been called in during one of the earlier stages, can let us down: the farther removed the planners are from the community where the program is to be put into action, the less effective will be their planning. Programs too hastily devised and based on too limited observations of a few self-chosen people frequently have to be changed later on; each unexpected change means added confusion and a loss of support for the program. Proper anticipation avoids later amputation.

Another group we should include in the planning includes those responsible for carrying out the planning. This sharing in the development and achievement of the program is necessary to the morale of the workers. Getting the help of people in the early stages makes them feel responsible for the success of the program, but more important, it gives them a say in what directly concerns them.

Since so many programs launched in a community are actually planned outside it, we need a special word about them. These programs may involve government planning or action in the state or national headquarters of an organization represented in the community.

The planning of a large-scale program can enlist the help of a much larger group of people than many suppose. It can extend from the highest official to the newest member, provided an important principle of organization is followed: the principle of determination of details at various levels. By asking those at each level (national, state, county, local) to make decisions about the details which operate on their level, the program gains momentum as it moves along.

In this connection it is interesting to notice that one of the largest religious bodies in the United States has adopted as an active policy the promotion of community-oriented programs by its members. The local groups of this church are studying ways to relate their religious activities to the needs of their own communities. Here and there surprising results are occurring.

The principle of determination of details at various

levels means that those initiating the program at the
top would fill in the general outlines of the program's
blueprints, but no more than absolutely necessary. The
outlines would then be passed on to the next level,
where further details would be added. And here would
occur the first variations. Some groups at this stage
would work out the program one way; other groups,
another way. But that is just what is necessary, for
only such an approach insures that the program is being adapted to the needs of the people of that area.
And so it goes on, until it reaches the local community.
Even here, the people should make some basic decisions, if only the choice of several plans.

The result will be that the program as put into action
in every local community will vary in many ways, but
there will be enough similarity, enough agreement on
basic principles, to give unity to a program of national
scope. Some communities may not think it necessary
to establish a new organization to carry out the program but will channel it through some group already
organized. This, of course, will sound like treason to
an administrator interested in perfecting a strong organization. But if he is willing to run roughshod over
the sensible people in such a community and insists
that only a new organization can do the job he has
in mind, he convicts himself in the eyes of the well
informed. He is more interested in an organization
that he can run than in the accomplishment of a program.

Another weakness of large-scale programs is that far
too many executives at the top want to work out the
complete blueprints before the program leaves their
offices. They don't distrust the local people, but they

have not learned how to delegate authority. Some also have the mistaken opinion that efficiency necessarily results from uniformity. It does not. In the field of organization, regional and local variations are necessary, or else there is a sterility in program endeavors that mystifies those who started things off with such high hopes of success. This weakness can be overcome on the local level, however. During the war I noted how the attempt at block organization failed in some communities where the leaders tried mechanically to follow the Washington blueprint. In other communities, considerable success resulted as the leaders adapted the Washington suggestions to their own circumstances.

If we are asked, then, to sponsor some large-scale program in our local community, we should find out how it came into being. Was it arrived at by careful deliberation of representative people? We should insist that we be allowed, with the help of other local people, to adapt the general plan to the specific needs of our community. This is not only good organization but also good motivation.

But more often we will be called upon to help in the planning of a local program. The choice of a first objective is important. It must fulfill at least these conditions.

1. *The first objective must be possible to achieve within a reasonable length of time,* so that people can derive a feeling of accomplishment without a great output of time and effort. So often workers start out to tackle the most difficult job in the community instead of choosing something simple which is related to the problem but which can be attacked and con-

quered. As members of the community gain experience and confidence in doing some of the least complicated tasks, they prepare themselves for the really difficult ones. Nothing succeeds like success.

2. *The first objective must be related to a need felt by members of the community.* It may not seem to go as far as many of them want to go, but it should at least seem in the right direction. There is quite a difference between the needs an outsider sees in a community and the needs which the local people want solved. Some communities prefer leisure to seeming efficiency, while others strive constantly to appear up to date and progressive. The objective, then, should be related to the important social values of the community. The fact-finding that was done should also have stressed the desirability of choosing this objective.

3. *The first objective should fit into a series of objectives, all leading toward the solution* of the major problem which prompted the program in the first place. That is, the plan should specify that—in the light of what we now know—we will do this first, then this, and then this, until the goal is achieved.

Having decided on our first objective, we must now include in our program how we are going about to achieve it. Every plan should provide for these needs.

1. How to explain the program to the public should be outlined in the program. Specifically, the plan should state what is to be told, what channels of communication are to be used to tell it, and who is responsible for seeing that it is told. In the next section more details will be given about specific techniques of getting this part of the job done, but the program should take this important phase into account.

2. After careful estimates have been made of the amount needed to finance the program, plans should be made for raising that amount. Solicitors should be decided upon, pledge cards printed, and a treasurer appointed. If relatively small amounts of money are to be handled, this phase need not be greatly detailed, but in no case should it be ignored in the hope that a Santa Claus will come through at the last moment.

3. Even before the money is raised, the planning group should know clearly how they are going to spend it. Someone well acquainted with the requirements of the project should help draw up a list of what material equipment and facilities will be needed to carry the program through to completion.

4. Finally, provision should be made for staffing the program when it calls for professional guidance. For instance, many communities make the grave mistake of building a playground without having any provision (or funds) for employing enough supervisors.

As soon as we have decided on the first task to undertake and have listed the necessary steps, we may proceed to the organizational phase. Various choices present themselves.

1. We may ask some organization already well established in the community to sponsor the program. Let's suppose, for instance, that a fact-finding survey on recreation revealed serious health deficiencies among the children and indicated that these should be given a priority over a playground or anything else. The Parent-Teacher Association or the local medical association or a men's service club with a long record of aiding children might be given the nod and asked to see this phase of the program through.

2. We may ask several established organizations and agencies to work jointly. This choice is particularly wise where more than one group has a vested interest in a line of activity and the chances for co-operation seem bright. Attempts to deal with juvenile delinquency, to cite but one case, frequently work best on this joint basis.

3. Finally, we may decide to set up a new organization. This is desirable particularly if two or more groups in conflict with each other claim a vested interest in the program under consideration. Members of each organization can take part in the new group, but as equals and not under the dominance of the rival club. In addition, enough new blood may be introduced into a new organization to decrease the friction which might result from such intergroup conflict.

We may also set up a new organization if no local groups have had much experience with anything similar to the proposed project. Once the planning group assures itself that it is truly representative, it may itself become the sponsoring body. Then it will be free to invite to its membership persons in the community whose support counts most. They can be made a part of the group and use their influence to good advantage. In other words, creating a new group gives us a chance to cut across existing organizational affiliations and get together a group of people best fitted for the service to be given.

A word of warning needs to be repeated. If the desire of a worker to set up a new organization (which will be under his control, at least in the beginning) makes him ignore the existence of a well-established group already associated in the public mind with the kind of job to be done, bypassing it purposely may prove a serious blunder as well as a waste of available human resources.

I recall the case of an executive secretary of a state welfare association who was able to put community welfare above her particular association. She was interested in the formation of local groups affiliated with her state organization, but always she asked first, "What kind of group can best promote social welfare in this community?" She found a number of communities already sufficiently organized and in no need of an extra group. She then gave her attention to gaining the support of the existing groups for the state-wide welfare efforts.

Although the next section discusses some of the specific means of winning over the public, any plan we make should set forth what steps are to be followed.

1. The planning group should agree on the kind of appeal that would prove most effective among the local people. This should be thrashed out thoroughly by those working up the program. Probably they will decide to open up several stops in the organ of persuasion.

2. Once the kind of appeal is agreed upon, we should appoint subcommittees to work out with the proper people the publicity to be accorded the program. One subcommittee could cover the press; another, the radio and television. A third could make plans for presenting the program before each organization and getting notices inserted in church bulletins; a fourth committee could discuss with school authorities the possibility that children carry information home to their parents; a fifth could see that the right slant on the program got into the gossip chain of the community.

Others could be appointed, depending upon how ambitious the undertaking proved to be and how actively various people were helping in its promotion. More details on some of these points will come later. (See Guidepost 20.) The work of these committees should be co-ordinated so that the publicity has a maximum effect through frequency, novelty, and a percolation down through all the social layers of the community.

With our program complete, we are ready for action. Let's look at how to launch it.

STAGE

4   *Launching the Program*

ALTHOUGH THE plan we discussed in the previous section has told us of some of the main points to consider in planning the program of action, its success or failure will depend upon how it is launched and how quickly it moves forward to one objective after another. One of the points listed there had to do with informing people about the program. Among the commonly used techniques which are in danger of being overlooked are these:

1. *The gossip chain.* In some communities I would rather have two talkative barbers reciting the virtues of my program for two or three days to all the customers who sat in their chairs than to have two or three high-sounding editorials in the local press. I won't deny the power of the press and the tremendous role it can wield in the formation of public opinion; it just so happens that getting the program favorably accepted in some of the community's gossip chains will aid greatly

in the launching. After all, the barber has his customer there at his mercy and can continue to clip hair or massage the scalp until all of the fine points of the program have been discussed. Nor is it unethical to win over a beauty operator to using some fresh angles of the program in lightening the conversation with the devotees of beauty committing themselves to her care. Every community has its loafing spots, such as the feed store, the courthouse, a fire station, or a bowling alley. Competent supporters in any of these places at the right times can be real assets.

2. *The dramatic trio.* Another technique involves what R. T. LaPiere in his book *Collective Behavior* terms the "dramatic trio" (hero, heroine, villain). The approach which an action group can make to the community is to represent itself as the hero out to save the community (the heroine) from the wiles or shame of the villain (the problem that needs correction). Skillful orators have long used this device to win votes or support for a cause. They usually make some opponent a villain, but manage to cast themselves in the role of the hero. Posters, news releases, public addresses can carefully work in variations of the dramatic trio theme as a legitimate means of appeal.

3. *Organizational meetings.* Speakers in behalf of the program may obtain a hearing before the hundred and one organized groups which are constantly on the search for program material. By presenting the message to people in groups, we are not putting them on the spot as individuals. A hesitant person, if he sees that those in the group seem to approve, will be likely to become a supporter too.

4. *Neighborhood meetings.* The evening that a pro-

gram is to be launched officially, it may be possible, in addition to the regular news stories, to arrange to have people all over the community gather in a school, church, or some other center nearest them to listen to a live broadcast from the studio of one (or all) of the local radio stations. This can explain in half an hour the purpose of the program, after which the neighborhood gatherings can be asked to discuss certain aspects of the plan which need immediate attention. The presiding officer at each neighborhood gathering can carry on at the end of the broadcast and invite public discussion. For instance, if the chief question at issue is the formation of a community council, each group can be asked to recommend to the temporary central committee how representation should be worked out, what problems they consider most immediate for a community council to study, and whether or not the council would be a clearinghouse, an action group, or both. Such gatherings mean considerable preparation by a committee for each neighborhood, but they prove one of the quickest and most effective ways of reaching many people simultaneously and giving them the story straight, while at the same time making them participants in the launching of the program.

But techniques in themselves have little value unless they lead to genuine motivation on the part of those concerned. In the case of a community program, some ways of ensuring motivation might be mentioned.

1. *Appeal to the self-interest of the people,* especially by threatening a pain in the pocketbook if the program falls through. Here is where the fact-finding will prove its worth, because figures can be quoted and evidence cited to show that success will cost less than failure.

2. *Assure the people that the program is theirs.* We can show them that a representative group has been working with the idea and the plan, and that these representatives are ready to reshape the plan as they are convinced that changes are required. We can maintain a two-way flow of ideas between the leaders and other people. To the degree that we as leaders conform to democratic practice, we find it easy to persuade the people that the program is in their own interest.

3. *Give credit freely,* but deservedly. Through the press and radio and in progress reports we ought to mention the names of those who have done superior jobs. The ordinary citizen possibly will identify himself with someone mentioned and receive a vicarious thrill.

4. *Make use of community loyalty and local pride.* We can tell accurately but emphatically what neighboring communities have done to improve their own conditions and challenge the citizens of our town to do them one better.

Anyone who has reflected seriously about the kind of town in which he lives can add a number of other ways of motivating his fellow townspeople to action. These suggestions simply are typical of the way leaders should guarantee deep motivation.

As circumstances arise, we ought to be willing to change the plan of action with the advice of all the others sharing primarily in the responsibility for the program. As a matter of fact, we should set the plan up in such a way that change is the expected thing. This can be done by planning for one objective at a time, as we discussed earlier, while having other suggestions ready for consideration as soon as a given objective has been achieved. If we can maintain this flexible state of mind, we will demonstrate a maturity of leadership that has carried us from the rooting of an idea to the stage of fact-finding in preparation for planning a program. We will show that we do not believe that the program, no matter how much work has gone into it, is an end in itself. Thus, we will be in the frame of mind to seek continually to keep up with the progress of the program.

STAGE

5   *Keeping Up With the Program*

WE SHOULD always know how the program is getting along. Nor do we need to be a master detective to keep ourselves informed. If we simply follow the practice of bringing up the subject of the program in enough different groups, then patiently listening, we can size up community sentiment.

1. We ought to know where we are in terms of the planned stages of the program. After all, a plan is meant to be followed unless, after deliberation, its details need to be changed in the light of new experience. So often a group which worked hard in forming a plan, saw it accepted and supposedly launched, finds out after a while that the leader is ignoring the plan, either purposely or inadvertently. We have an obligation to those who worked up the plan, since in many cases, particularly where publicity has been given, the prestige of those in on the planning will rise or fall with the fortunes of the program. Those in the know sometimes divulge steps in the plan to some of their

intimates and find it quite embarrassing to see these steps never materialize, with no explanation offered by the person responsible. Earlier plans may need to be changed, but they should not be ignored.

2. We should know what rough spots need immediate attention. Some person with a major responsibility may be away from town for three weeks and may not make provision for his job during his absence. We should either step into the gap or have someone else in mind to take over. Or again, some committee chairman may complain that he cannot carry his work forward until some others do their assignment. Here we should see if we can speed the lagging persons along. This means that in the beginning we should not tie ourselves down to some routine part of the program, but should keep ourselves free to smooth over rough spots as they are met.

3. We ought to be sure that those helping us are getting satisfying training for leadership. A thorough-going community program under democratic leadership will wind up with many potential leaders better trained and more self-confident. Our role as a leader, therefore, is not that of barking out orders to heel-clicking subordinates, but rather that of discussing the program in process so that those who take part will get a clearer insight into the community and into the way people can accomplish a project together. This principle applies particularly to the professional leader who has come into the community. He should try to work himself out of a job—at least as far as any given program is concerned. To the extent that local people take it over, he is free to begin other projects; or if he travels from one community to another, he need

spend less time in the one where local leaders are being made available.

4. As we keep up with the program and know just what phase it is passing through, we can take time to think about what's coming next. We can do that now, not later on when quick action suddenly is demanded. In the light of where we are now, we begin to anticipate what we will do next. With the effective leader, the future is very much a part of the present.

Since we have managed to keep ourselves from becoming involved deeply in the detailed administration of the program (because we have known how to delegate responsibility to others) we will take time to evaluate the progress made to date. We know, among other things, these matters.

1. We must issue frequent reports, but only when we have some achievement to announce. Too much talk about what we are going to do, no matter how pious or fervent the expression, falls flat after a while.

2. We must decide what to chalk up to experience. Frequently, there are disappointments, mistakes, and even failures. Each of these experiences, if properly analyzed, could add to our knowledge of do's and don'ts in community organization. It is a sad mistake to brood over what went wrong. Once whatever happened has been thought through carefully, we should write it off the ledger and put our energies into more pressing tasks at hand. Of course, the leader who blithely blames every error upon an unfriendly Lady Luck is really hiding behind her skirts, an occupation hardly befitting a gentleman.

3. We must assess our helpers and decide what their chief contributions and strong points have been. Those

who don't blame themselves or Lady Luck may blame their assistants. We should realize that many people are pressed into doing a community job through loyalty and a desire to serve. So often the square pegs are assigned the round holes. The fault in such a case is not the peg but the one who made the assignment. Frequently reassessing the best kind of help certain people can give is a part of taking our bearings in the light of where we have been.

4. We ought to use a community check sheet. If such sheets have been used in the beginning stages, they can be used after action has been under way to chart progress—the before-and-after technique. If check sheets were not available in the beginning, they nevertheless can be a means of showing what still lies ahead. That is, a running account of progress to date can be climaxed by a check sheet emphasizing the necessity of keeping our shoulder to the wheel. A community-centered school, for example, may be interested in improving the diet, housing (screens, toilet facilities), street beautification, library facilities, and so on. A scorecard quickly shows what the situation was at different dates, thus measuring the progress that has been made. (See Guidepost 4.)

Every program should have an end, as we have already noted. We should look forward to reaching this destination and bend our energies toward that goal. It is well for us as leaders bringing the program to completion to be aware of these important points.

1. Few programs ever are achieved 100 per cent. To be sure, financial drives may go over the top in total amount raised, but along the way there were some substantial citizens from whom no contribution

came. Whenever it seems that the last small part of the project is going to call for much greater effort than the value received, we must be ready to wind up the program with good grace. Let's concentrate rather on the 90 per cent that was accomplished and answer our critics that 90 per cent is considerably better than nothing, which would have been the box score if the program had never been conducted.

2. Communities can sustain interest in a project only so long. We may remain intently interested, but the public likes to shift its attention from one thing to another. In the spring its emphasis may be on getting new baseball uniforms for the stalwart sluggers of the community; in an election year it may be willing to listen to talk about honest elections and may even support a clean politics campaign; in late summer or early fall a county fair may absorb most of the people's spare energy. Our program then must take these cycles of interest into account. We must rely upon variety to quicken any dimming enthusiasm, but we cannot let the program drag on and on beyond the possibility of resuscitation.

3. There is nothing sacred about a program as such. After consulting with those who did the planning and those aiding in its execution, we should give it a new look as frequently as the occasion demands. Of course, we won't resort to these tactics simply to keep the program alive for the sake of having a program, but in order to gain for the community something the people need and want. No program should be an end, but simply a means to an end.

4. The creative experience shared by those who took part should be emphasized. Neighbors who helped

at a barn-raising when looking at the barn later on don't say to themselves, "Look at the barn! Isn't it nice that Bill Perkins has a new barn!" Instead, in pointing to the barn they say, "Look at what a bunch of us fellows did one day. Had the biggest time you ever saw." In other words, it was the creative, shared experience that proved satisfying. So it is with programs in communities both large and small. As a matter of fact, the larger the community the more often we will hear people say, "One of the most enjoyable features of helping with that program was meeting so many interesting and stimulating people."

As the program draws to a close, we must be sure that it leaves a good taste with those who helped, so that they will be ready to help on other projects when their services are requested again. A gala social affair, carefully planned to make even the least sophisticated participant feel at home, is often a fitting way to wind up a program.

This section of the book will have accomplished its purpose if it has shown us the need for going about community leadership systematically instead of impetuously. So many of us—and this is particularly true of community workers—live in a world of pressures. We have more to do within our waking hours than we can get done comfortably, and so we do those things to which our attention is most forcibly and persistently called. In such a hectic atmosphere, anything as intangible as a community program may be pushed aside and receive only the crumbs of our time. It is important, therefore, that what time we do give be well directed, to the point, and that each successive endeavor build on what has gone before. If we take up one stage at a time and give it our concentration, even though it be for a limited period, we will be surprised what we can actually accomplish. We will find, however, the leadership of a community program both distracting and fatiguing if we have to concern ourselves with scores of details, one after the other, without seeing how each detail fits into the general scheme and adds up significantly in the total effort.

Some readers may be disappointed not to find in this section such headings as: If you want to promote a Girl Scout cookie sale in your community, what are the cut-and-dried, tried-and-true steps to follow? Or, if you are trying to work out a program of co-operation between two rival churches, what is the one, two, three of that? The more such readers turn to this book, read it, and use it, the more they will see the greater value in possessing a fund of general knowledge out of which they can fashion specific plans for each given situation. The danger of using a cut-and-dried approach, supposedly applicable to all communities, is that once a given step in the sequence does not go as expected, the whole effort collapses.

In our leadership, therefore, we will see a community program in its entirety as it goes through the stages of promotion:

1. Rooting the idea,
2. Getting the facts,
3. Planning a program,
4. Launching the program, and
5. Keeping up with the program.

But we will do more than that. We will see the program against the background of our community. And since the program must be achieved through some organization already existing or specially created for the purpose, we will see how groups can be used effectively in carrying out a community program. And it is with the discussion of group mechanics—how to make our group more effective—that the next part of this handbook is concerned.

HOW TO MAKE OUR GROUP EFFECTIVE: SEVEN AREAS

AN ORGANIZED group is a great deal like a car. It consists primarily of a number of parts put together according to some plan. It exists—or should exist—not as an end in itself but to get something done. Such a group, like a car, has to have power or drive to move it along. When it moves, it has to head in some direction, have some goal or destination. Then, too, it has a braking system which may work too well, rather well, or not well enough. An organization, like an automobile which gets out of control, can do much damage. It may ignore the rights of others and the rules of the community, thereby causing much harm.

The creation of a new group, like the purchase of a new automobile, may be prompted by a variety of motives. For some reason, those interested in a certain program, whether they are local or outside leaders, may consider the launching of a new group preferable either to working on an informal, unorganized basis or to using groups already in existence. They may then get people together to begin the round of organizational activity, which includes the preparation of a statement of purpose and the election of officers.

Why do leaders work through groups? For one thing, we Americans are organization-minded. Large numbers of us have a hankering to belong to many different groups and wear the insignia to which our membership entitles us. It is just part of our way of life.

But organizations have quite definite advantages.

1. An organization provides mutual stimulation among the members. The greater the number of people working on a topic, the broader will be the social experience brought to bear on that topic. Someone has said, "If I give you a dollar and you give me a dollar, we each will still have one dollar. But if I give you an idea and you give me an idea, then we each have two ideas."

2. An organization fixes certain responsibilities and duties both upon its officers and its members. For example, a man elected to a club office knows that the members will expect him to do the job the leader is supposed to do. He in turn can call upon the members for assistance and advice, since they are expected to live up to their part of the bargain. Thus, through organization, people can be more certain that specific jobs will be done.

3. An organization, through bestowal of its honored positions, can recognize services rendered, past and present, by certain of its members. This is a spur to increased activity on the part of many persons.

4. An organization gives continuity to a program since it provides for one set of officers to succeed another and for self-renewal in the taking in of new members.

5. Forming an organization gives public recognition

to programs, because most people upon learning of a new group will ask what it has set out to do. When a national organization, for instance, establishes a local group and publicizes its formation, people begin to ask, "What is this new group trying to do?" Those doing the organizing, then, have an opportunity to explain; they can get their point of view before the public. (See Guidepost 20.)

Formal organizations often have distinct disadvantages, however, for getting certain jobs done.

1. An informal group at times may assure the cooperation of everyone on a more equal footing. Electing officers may permit those who hold no positions to settle back and let the leaders do the work. It is easy, indeed, to let George do it, even though George is a much busier person than most of the other members.

2. An organization may meet the opposition of vested interests or of other groups already strongly established. An informal group, however, may carry on its activities unopposed and eventually win wide support for its unofficial program.

3. If the activity is of a short-run nature and must be accomplished quickly, there is no need to give it the permanence implied in a formal organization. The time used in organizational activity could better be spent on an informal basis with key leaders who are willing to work hard and act promptly.

4. In some communities, people do not have a good record of working together in organizations. Formal groups often become debating societies where more friction than co-operation results. This is especially true where the community is sharply divided into various factions.

5. People representing different groups and interests often can work out programs requiring compromise much better on an informal basis. If they speak in an organizational meeting, they must speak for public consumption; that is, they must be the spokesmen for the groups they supposedly represent in the community. They may even assume a fighting pose which they do not show in a private gathering. Once they have committed themselves in public, they find it difficult to back down. As a case in point, those interested in improving the relationships between races have found that an informal meeting of representatives of the two groups accomplishes much more than would an organization launched at a large meeting where everybody is asked to speak his mind. (See Guidepost 8.)

These lists of advantages and disadvantages, although they do not tell the whole story, should help us to think through the question of why form a new group. We should keep in mind that there is always the possibility of working through some existing organization to good advantage. But whether we are setting up a new group or are working with one already established, we will want to make our group more effective in at least these seven areas:

1. Leader-group relations,
2. Group drive,
3. Membership qualifications,
4. Procedures,
5. Finances,
6. Meetings, and
7. Committees.

Of these, the most important is the leader's attitude toward the group.

1   *Leader-Group Relations*

How EFFECTIVE a group will be depends greatly upon how effective a relationship exists between leaders and followers. A leader who speaks of a group as "mine" thereby implies that he expects the members

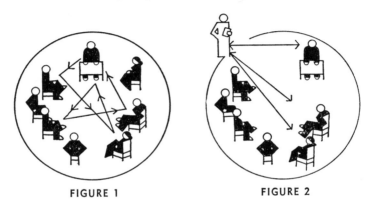

FIGURE 1   FIGURE 2

to do what he says. Possessiveness is just as common a failing among leaders as it is among parents; so is overprotection and a feeling that one's way is the only right way of doing things.

The experienced leader likes to see the group members themselves tackle problems and reach independent conclusions. He expects them to speak of "our organization." If he is outside the group, he knows that when it stands on its own feet, he can devote his attention to other groups or to other problems. He is always ready to advise, but as far as possible he tries to help others learn to help themselves. If he is an officer of the group, he knows that people are being trained to take his place in the organization when his term of office is up.

Leader-group relations take different forms which vary in their relative efficiency.

1. When people who are well acquainted form an organization, the leadership usually comes from and responds to the followers. This democratic relationship

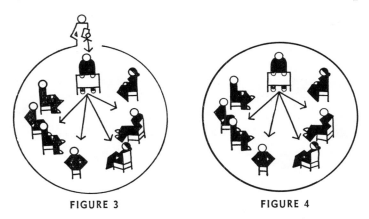

FIGURE 3   FIGURE 4

is shown in Figure 1. Here we see that the members are in touch not only with each other but with their leaders as well. They influence and are influenced by their leaders. In the long run, this type of relationship is the most efficient, because it builds up a much better feeling of loyalty to the organization and so assures greater likelihood of wholehearted participation in the group's activities. In this relationship all followers can become leaders at one time or another, and all leaders are followers in certain circumstances. Hence, everyone gets both leader and follower experience. Groups having a minimum of outside help generally work this way. People carry out activities upon which they agree; they more willingly follow leaders whom they elect and with whom they feel in accord.

2. The second type of leader-group relations is the manipulated sort. Actual leadership lies in the manipulator outside the group rather than in the officers. In Figure 2 we can see the gap between officers and members; and in Figure 3 the influence exerted by the manipulator through the officers upon the members. Furthermore, the members are not in association. Some manipulators keep control in their own hands and often are unwilling to delegate authority to others. The organization remains a one-man affair, falling apart as soon as the manipulator withdraws, for the motivation comes from outside. Other manipulators train officers and members, since they realize that manipulation is merely a preparatory stage to the development of the democratic relationship.

3. Other organizations come into being when one, two, or three people get enthusiastic about an idea and get themselves elected officers of some hastily formed group. Such an organization arouses the suspicions of many people, because they have the feeling that the officers are using the members as instruments for carrying out their original purpose, which may be either benevolent or selfish. Such officers take little time to keep the members informed and spend even less time discovering the followers' wishes. The organization in Figure 4 exists for the officers and not for the members. The leader-group influences move just one way— from the top down. Such a relationship is good in an emergency, when the people want to be told what to do, but its advantages quickly vanish when the crisis is past.

Although the democratic relationship between leader and group is without question the most efficient of the three types, sincere people set forth at least three objections to it. These criticisms are not well founded, but we can use them to point out the advantages of the democratic approach over the other two kinds.

1. "The leader loses control of what the group can do" is the first criticism. It is indeed true that group behavior, especially where there is much uninformed discussion, does result in rather strange things. But the democratic leader still can influence group thinking without dominating it. His chief task is to inform, to educate the key persons in the group to the steps that need to be taken, and then trust them to go ahead. Ideas which may have originated with him become the ideas of the members when they discuss them, change them as they see fit, and then act upon them in a businesslike way. We should recognize the fact, frequently overlooked, that the members themselves have many splendid ideas. We simply have to choose between working with the group or working on the group. If we choose the first type, we really become educators; otherwise, we become manipulators.

2. "If everything is left up to the local members, we cannot get uniformity in our local groups throughout the country" is a second criticism of the democratic approach. National officers may be so interested in standardization that they are willing to override community and cultural variations. If so, they will of necessity have to manipulate and dominate. If, however, they want each local community to carry out in the best possible way some activity or program, they will prefer the democratic approach.

3. A third complaint often heard about the democratic approach is "It takes too much time to set up an organization of this sort." But does it? If a person who is not a permanent member of a group tries to encourage the development of the mutual relationship, he does have to spend more time informing the people of what the program involves, gain their co-operation, and then suggest that they set up their organization with their own leaders. He probably will go as far as to suggest to them the type of organization which will do the job best and advise about other matters which seem in order. But he will stress the point that the organization belongs to the members and that they are the ones who will carry out the program. They make the final decisions for which they accept responsibility. Even local leaders, who are a part of the group, gain in the long run by not being in a hurry.

But the manipulative approach has its appeal. It seems less of an effort, and much of it can be done at an office desk. The professional promoter can get the names of a few likely leaders, notify them by letter of their appointment, write to those eligible for membership that so-and-so leaders have been appointed, and then try to get everybody together later on for an organizational meeting. There may be quite a large gathering at first, but under this type of leader-group relationship interest soon begins to wane. If the group is to last, someone must educate the people to see the need for the organization and must foster an understanding relationship between leaders and followers. This particular task usually takes longer than would have the slower preparation called for by the democratic type, and thus may not save time at all.

It often happens that a community leader, whether president of a PTA or a county agent, is pressed for reports on his organizational activity. He has to trump up something in a hurry, and the manipulated group is the product. Later, he has to work night and day to make the group into one that really gets things done. Sometimes he fails completely. He succeeds to the extent that he is able to change the organization into something approaching the democratic type.

Quite often the person promoting the program, if not altogether familiar with the local situation, can discover the best leaders for a certain activity by talking to a number of people. He can arrive at a general agreement on the basis of which he can appoint leaders. But in doing this he has observed a basic principle of organization: he has chosen leaders with whom the followers are already in the desired relationship and did not simply select people whom, because they were willing to follow him, seemed to him to be good leaders.

We have already seen that it is possible to change from one type of leader-group relations to another. Let's suppose that the group we are working with is already organized as the manipulated type. What can we do to create the democratic leader-follower relationship?

1. We can help the members understand the need for the program.

2. We can help them see how group action would aid in the program.

3. We can convince ourselves, the temporary officers, and potential members that the manipulated type is only a partial step in group organization.

4. When this understanding is general, then we can

suggest that the members select as official leaders those whom they want to guide the group in this activity.

5. If we plan to remain outside the group, we will interfere little with the leader-group relations thus created, but let both officers and members know that we are ready to advise on any problems that come up and that we will leave the responsibility of decision with the group.

Unfortunately, the known cases of changing the domineering approach to the democratic are so few that we cannot with our present knowledge trace the most effective steps which the transformation should follow. Those who have enjoyed such authority seldom give it up willingly; members who have been rather blind followers accept responsibility with reluctance. These facts account for the difficulty of changing the dominated type to the mutual leader-group relationship.

AREA

2   *Group Drive*

A GROUP HAS to move in some direction, or else it dies and is forgotten. Over and over again people are asked to set up an organization, which they obligingly do, only to learn that those who initiated the group have nothing important for it to do. When these people are asked why they wanted the group in the first place, they say, "Oh, we wanted to have the people organized just in case we needed their help later on." Without realizing it, they were making it difficult to gain co-operation when the time for assistance came. For group life implies activity. This activity comes from some drive or interest that holds the members of the group together and makes them work to accomplish the group purpose.

1. The drive may be largely internal. Here the interest of the members in what they are doing is so keen that they pay little attention to outside opinion and pressures. What they are doing is so much fun, seems so worth while, and may even be so exciting that the group activity is its own reward. At times, the leaders exert such an influence over their followers that the chief drive on the part of the members comes from the desired association with, and rendering service to, the leaders. This, however, is only secondarily a group process, and one that won't last when the leader is gone.

2. External forces may also add to the group drive. If a club is given an assignment by the community, the members feel that they must come through in order to maintain the group's prestige. Some groups are jealous of their standing in the community, and because they have been highly successful in past undertakings, bend every effort to be successful again. If, too, a group is threatened by outsiders, the members draw more closely together, become more conscious of the common bond that unites them in the face of a hostile environment. Consequently, they are motivated more keenly to make their organization strong.

3. But generally, the group drive is both internal and external. The goal to be achieved, the interests of the members, the devotion of the leaders, the influence of public opinion, and the past history of the group all help to give the group whatever drive it develops.

Drive alone is not enough to keep a group alive. Where the purpose of the organization is not clearly understood, there is floundering or a considerable waste of energy. Group after group has died prematurely because the leaders did not state what the group was supposed to do. Often the goals of a group are changed as time goes on; this, indeed, is almost necessary for group survival.

In almost every organization some members are more advanced in their thinking than others who do not keep up to date their ideas of what the organization should accomplish. Frequently, these conservative members serve as effective brakes on what would otherwise turn out to be rash plunging ahead, but sometimes they merely hold back. In such case, we should be realistic in raising the question of whether the organization still has a right to continue functioning in the community. We should do whatever we can to keep the people informed of the necessity for change and the part they can play in bringing about some new program.

Often leaders ask, "What can we do to get members interested in our organization?" If there is some important community need that is not being met and in which the members would take an intelligent interest, we should by all means take up the new activity. If nothing of this sort is available, we should let the group dissolve; it has probably outlived its usefulness. Many groups need a burial rather than an attempted rejuvenation.

AREA

3   *Membership Qualifications*

FROM THE beginning of time, birds of a
feather have flocked together.   There is no reason,
therefore, to wonder at the behavior of those who,
upon starting a group, want to admit only those who
think and act like themselves.   That is why they set
up rigid qualifications for membership.   These qualifications, based on social and economic factors, give the
group an exclusiveness which makes it more important
in the eyes of those who are in, and often makes it seem
more important to those on the outside.

Of course, what is exclusive in one community may
not seem at all exclusive in another, so widely do the
social values—what people consider important—vary
from one part of the country to the other.   We should
understand, however, the advantages and disadvantages
of having what the community considers an exclusive
group.

1. If the leaders of an organization set up specific
bars to membership, they make fairly certain that the
group will consist of people with a common background
in certain things.   To say that members of a milk pro-
ducers' co-operative have to meet requirements of size
of herd, amount of milk produced, and health standards
limits the membership to those of a certain economic
level.   The small farmer is not eligible for membership;
therefore, the policies of the group tend to further the
interests of those who represent financial success.   Or,
to restrict a woman's group, such as the American
Association of University Women, to women with col-

lege training is one way of getting together a group of women with something in common.

2. Exclusiveness also gives an organization prestige if the qualifications are connected with the community's standard of what is important. This prestige, together with the common interests among the members, means that the group, even if originally begun by some outside person, can run on its own power. The members agree on objectives, and the group drive is strengthened.

3. But what a community might term exclusiveness has its disadvantages. If the organization is considered snobbish, then many people outside the group view it with suspicion. The result is likely to be a much more limited contribution to community life. Too much emphasis on social or economic distinctions may create community cleavages and keep the people conscious of unhealthy social differences. In addition, many persons join such groups simply to gain personal prestige and not to contribute wholeheartedly to the group's enterprises. There is also the danger that two or three exclusive groups in a small community may draw off the best leadership and finances from organizations less exclusive but engaged in community-wide services. Those who do not gain admittance to the highly prized organizations have little social participation as a result.

AREA
4 *Procedures*

LEADERS ARE often faced with the problem of determining standardized procedures for regular meetings as well as the impressive ceremonies that many organizations have for the installation of officers and the initiation of new members. These, like membership qualifications, have their helpful as well as their possible harmful effects.

1. Much awkwardness and embarrassment is avoided in a group where everybody through the use of standardized procedures knows how each person is supposed to behave. New members in particular can quickly learn ritual and so make their contribution to the work of the group sooner than if they had had to become acquainted with the behavior of each member before they took an active part.

2. Ritualistic procedures also lessen the differences between qualified and unqualified officers. Less experienced officers can use ritual to carry the group through situation after situation in an acceptable way. Without some prescribed procedures, they would be helpless on many occasions.

Opening a meeting in a customary way, for example, quickly gets the members quieted and into the proper frame of mind, especially if they have been trained to take certain roles once the ceremony is begun. A salute to the flag, the singing of the National Anthem, the repetition of an organizational creed are ritualistic and serve useful group purposes in transferring to the group the patriotic and religious feelings already deep-rooted in the membership. This does not mean that a leader should exploit patriotism, let us say, for some unworthy objective; it simply recognizes the love of country as a basic social drive and provides for the expression of this drive in a group situation. (See Guidepost 17.)

In spite of these advantages, there are some dangers in the use of ritual.

1. Although ritual gives direction and stability to a group, it also tends to keep an organization alive that, from the community standpoint, should have folded up long ago. Perhaps the organization has outlived its period of usefulness, but a few members may have become so entranced by the intricacies of ritual that they try to keep the group going for that alone. Certainly it is serving a recreational purpose for these enthusiasts, but that is the extent of its usefulness.

2. At times preoccupation with group procedures, even in the early stages of organization, hinders the achievement of stated group purposes greatly in need of fulfillment. The original goal is forgotten, and standardization itself becomes the end rather than the means. This becomes readily apparent when at some meeting the chairman makes a fetish of Roberts' *Rules of Order* and when parliamentary law is a matter of more discussion than the real business at hand. (See Guidepost 19.)

3. Some ritual is useful, but too much of it is distracting. The degree to which it is used will have to depend upon community and cultural variations. At any rate, the exact amount cannot be prescribed satisfactorily in the headquarters of some national organization and still be best adapted to the needs of each locality throughout the country.

A R E A
5
Finances

MOST ORGANIZATIONS will have several problems connected with money. Whether the group decides upon regular dues, periodic assessments, money-raising schemes, or a combination of these depends upon the type of program it wants to sponsor. Even though problems vary from organization to organization, there are some practices which are used widely.

1. The group should adopt a budget for the use of all anticipated funds. Group life is not enriched particularly when a treasurer stands up to say, "We have an extra ten dollars in the treasury. What shall we do with it?" Generally, everybody has a different idea, and over the course of a year or two, fairly large sums can be spent in a hit-or-miss fashion. Long-term planning, acted upon by the whole group, is desirable, but it should not, of course, be an end in itself.

2. The members should feel that they have the say-so regarding the amounts they pay. An autocratic edict from the executive committee or an arbitrary amount determined by some outside district or national office may injure group morale considerably. Quite often the same end can be achieved by a request rather than an order from above. If the members of a local club believe that outside representatives of the organization are rendering them a service, they will usually contribute willingly enough.

3. A money-raising campaign for some such cause as the purchase of a new church carpet or the collection of funds for war relief is often the only activity during the year in which every member has a chance to participate. A well-planned campaign which uses each person may be a morale-builder of the first order. Too frequent campaigns, however, quickly result in loss of interest on the part of those who carry the load.

4. The collection and expenditure of funds should be so well controlled that the members can know at any time how the group stands financially. The statements should be simple and the accounts examined regularly.

5. A group Santa Claus or some well-intentioned person who underwrites all organizational expenses may prove a detriment rather than a help. Other members under such circumstances often leave not only finances but also important decisions to such a person. They even hesitate to take any action which they fear might meet with Santa's disapproval. This curtails discussion and freedom of group action. It also tends to eliminate the group struggle for a goal which welds the officers and members into a successful team.

6. Poor attendance at meetings often results because many members have not paid their dues and are so far in arrears that they feel uncomfortable while attending. Over and over again we will find such people still much interested in the work of the organization but apologetic because they are behind in their payments. Perhaps it may even seem wise to lower the amount of dues. When a large number of members are in arrears, the group may choose to cancel all unpaid dues and start out with a clean slate.

A word about group finances and the community! It is well to remember that in many towns the people feel that the financial support of the existing organizations seriously taxes their economic resources. On the other hand, it has been found again and again that adequate financial support can be obtained easily for community projects from public-spirited citizens if they see the value of a certain activity. Satisfactions from community improvement in which the people take pride are quite as real as those from individual expenditures for personal enjoyment. Many well-to-do people have not invested in the community life because leaders have not shown the importance of their programs. In the lower income groups, too, a majority will help, each according to his ability. After all, community accomplishments yield deep satisfaction to the persons who help bring them about.

If we would be successful leaders, we will think of finances as we do of ritual: as a means to an end. We will ask these questions: What do we as a group want to do, how much money will it take, and how will we raise that amount? The answers we will leave to the members themselves.

A R E A

6   *Meetings*

WHAT WOULD the members of the group we are interested in customarily reply when a wife or husband asked them, "What did you do at the meeting tonight?" Would the answer be, "Oh, Mr. Fuss Budget talked for half an hour about something he didn't know anything about and then Mr. I. Makem Squirm took up the other half hour, after which I came home"? Or would the member be able to state explicitly in a sentence or two just what had been accomplished? This suggests the first of meeting helps. (See Guidepost 17.)

1. Meetings should achieve some objective that the group believes important. If people are getting together to have a good time, then they should have a good time. If they have to face an important organiza-

tion problem, then they should limit themselves to small enough phases of the problem so that they can take definite action about something before they adjourn.   In fact, the person in charge should state at the end of the meeting just what has been done and what remains to do, putting the matter in such a way that the members leave with the feeling that they have spent their time well.   Mere discussion in the hope that somebody will have a brilliant idea which the others will find to their liking is a poor excuse for coming together.

2. Members should know in advance why they are meeting.   This avoids the long warm-up period that many uninformed members have to undergo as well as the useless discussion that accompanies it.   It means also that the officers will be less likely to confront the membership suddenly with a proposal and get it enacted before people have had a chance to decide what they want to do about it.   Furthermore, it means that in a good meeting the items of business will be such that they can be discussed from all angles and decided in the time allowed.   Where meetings are a mixture of business and pleasure, both purposes should be served.

3. Much time is wasted in meetings discussing items that should be entrusted to committees or even individuals.   The kind of ice cream that should be served at the Fourth of July picnic is important in a way, but hardly deserves ten minutes of debate in an hour meeting at which many are in attendance and when there are other things to consider.

4. Another test of a good meeting is the extent to which the various members have a chance to take part.

The complaint about Mr. Fuss Budget is only too common. As a result, the person who attends feels that he might just as well have stayed at home. Large participation calls for planning. It does not mean that every member should be called on for a speech, but it does mean that anyone with anything to say should have a chance to say it.

5. Again, the one responsible for the meeting must expect variations in meeting practices. Some audiences assemble with the idea of being entertained. Others like to have a speaker make his remarks, then sit down and give them time to think about what was said. There is variation, too, in who attends meetings. In some places whole family groups are present, while in others only the men attend.

AREA 7 *Committees*

COMMITTEES CAN be useful tools to get an organization's work done. They can provide for participation by all the members. But committees have their dangers, too.

1. Many organizations have too many committees that never accomplish anything. This is especially true of those bodies trying to conform to an organizational plan worked out in some national headquarters without regard for community variations. Many groups could get along admirably with a program committee, provided special committees did specific jobs as needs arose. Such special committees should last only as long as the particular task requires.

2. Some groups tend to place the same people on committees over and over again. These wheel horses do get the work done, but greater effort should be taken to team them up with less experienced people so that more people will be taking part and thus the organization strengthened.

3. Some officers think of a committee as a device to forestall some action of which they disapprove. If some member suggests an idea which the chairman does not like, he may appoint a committee to look into the matter, hoping that the idea will die in committee. The fair-minded leader may use the same committee technique, but with this difference: he will appoint a strong committee consisting perhaps of the originator of the idea, some person who is likely to disagree, and someone else known to have not made up his mind on the matter. He will also call for a committee report in due course of time, for he knows that nothing kills effective committee work more quickly than the frustration that comes from working hard on a problem and then having the committee report filed without so much as a hearing.

4. Much too often, the officers adopt a committee's recommendations and do not state the names of those responsible for the recommendations. If recognition is given for the work a committee has done, other committees will do a better job. (See Guidepost 18.)

In the long run, however, how effective a group may be in community work does not depend entirely upon how well it runs. An organization may have the highest degree of efficiency in the seven areas we have discussed:

1. Leader-group relations,
2. Group drive,
3. Membership qualifications,
4. Procedures,
5. Finances,
6. Meetings, and
7. Committees,

and yet be considered lifeless by nonmembers. What we have seen about each of these areas applies equally well to the group: its end is community service. We as community-minded leaders ought to be aware, therefore, of the place of the group in community life.

1. Groups do not exist alone. They are part and parcel of the community and frequently take on a decidedly local flavor. They conform to local practice in such simple matters as starting or not starting on time, serving refreshments at meetings, and the prominence given women in organizational life.

2. Furthermore, each group has a certain status in the community, of which its members are quite conscious. It is a decided honor to belong to some organizations, while other groups rank lower in the opinion of the people of the community. In a real sense, the spirit within a group is likely to rise as the status of the group rises in the community. Organizations frequently adopt community projects to improve their standing; they invite as members people with prestige and sometimes exclude those who are looked upon unfavorably by the town. On the other hand, should the group feel threatened or seem to suffer the disapproval of the community, that may serve as a bond drawing the members close together, temporarily at least. But in the long pull, those groups which con-

form to community standards last the longest and prove the most satisfying to their members.

3. Organizations may also be classed by the interest they show in community affairs. Some are definitely civic in nature and devote considerable energy to community improvement and to the training of their members for broad participation as citizens. Others concern themselves with leisuretime activities, although these have a bearing on what the community considers proper. There are certain organizations, particularly those based on genealogical background, which are culture bearing and which are thought by members to enhance their local prestige. Often, when these organizations undertake community activities, they bring to bear upon them a weight of influence which proves a considerable aid.

Frequently organizational leaders take up projects which seem important to a few members of the group, but they do not ask carefully whether or not the people of the community consider these projects important. They forget that their organization is a part of the community and must work within its social values. The more we as leaders keep in touch with the actual state of mind of the community, the more sensitive we will be to the desires of the community at large and the importance of guiding our organization into actual usefulness. Just how effective our group will then be depends largely upon what is our philosophy of community service.

OUR PHILOSOPHY
OF CIVIC SERVICE:
FIVE QUESTIONS

MUCH OF THE emphasis of this handbook has been upon techniques, ways of getting the job done. But techniques of themselves are sterile. When used by the ignorant and uninformed, they may prove dangerous; when used by the selfish and unscrupulous, they may prove vicious. They become community assets only when they are employed intelligently by civic leaders who are genuinely interested in giving service.

It becomes necessary, therefore, that we who are engaged in community activities should bring to our tasks a mature philosophy of community service. Of course, we cannot adopt such a philosophy ready-made from someone else, but we can consider the ideas of others when forming our own approach. Here are some of the questions that deserve thinking over and which can prove starting points as we look over our own reasons for taking part in community activities of various kinds.

1. What is a community?
2. What is the basis of community life?
3. How should knowledge be used?
4. How should we look at change?

5. What is our part in community service?
If we can answer these questions to our own satisfaction, we will have a sound basis on which to build a mature philosophy of community service.

QUESTION

1   *What Is a Community?*

WHETHER WE wish to study human nature or the traits of society at large, we do not have to wander far from our own front door. In our own communities we will find a crisscross of interacting personalities revealing the heights and depths of which humanity is capable; we will see also in our own home town the same forces at work which commentators at the United Nations headquarters describe on an international scale. This is not to say that the best student of human nature is the least traveled student, but to every observing person his own community can prove a fascinating drama.

But what is a community after all? That question is often asked, and quite properly so. Since no single definition, neatly condensed into three or four sentences, conveys the idea, it is more helpful to indicate some of the chief characteristics which every community possesses. In a sense, this will be a review of many sections of the handbook.

1. A community is an area which can be mapped. It includes those people who feel a sense of belonging to a certain center, such as a village, a town, a city. It is particularly important to remember that this area is usually not identical with any political unit, since

community boundaries tend to spill over city limits or even across county lines. Community councils or other such groups, therefore, concern themselves quite often with two or more governmental units (city and county) when working out some community-wide project. Community maps are used to ensure wide geographical representation in community activities. (See Guidepost 2.)

2. A community's welfare depends upon adequate use of the advantages of its location and of its natural resources. Sound planning for community improvement calls for detailed consideration of soil productivity, extraction of minerals, scientific cutting of timber, harnessing of water power, and development of favorable transportation features. In other words, a community is more than an area; it is an area with distinctive geographical and resource features.

3. A community is a service center. People gain a sense of community as they share the same services: stores, banks, movies, doctors, utilities, churches, schools, transportation facilities, and all the other conveniences now available in the average town. A community, then, is a place where people shop, where they work for their living, where they get professional services, and where they find recreation. It includes rural families, for the decreasing self-sufficiency of even the farm population increases the dependence upon the service center and gives country folk an attachment to those towns where they are made to feel at home. Population changes, whether in terms of total numbers, proportion of men to women, children to adults, or actively employed to aged, affect markedly the clientele of these community services. (See Guidepost 3.)

4. A community is also a set of social relationships. It is already organized to get things done. Clubs and organizations exist, and informal groups gossip, have fun, and help mold public opinion. Community workers should use the existing social arrangements as much as possible.

5. Community leadership takes on the complexion of the local social traits. Among other things, it is associated with whatever class system is present.

6. Every community to a greater or lesser degree has community loyalty. When people identify their own interests with those of a total community, they are more inclined to pay less attention to those smaller loyalties that divide the townspeople. Many community workers are able to find agreement activities about which good neighborliness can develop and give people the feeling of doing something together. The community with greatest loyalty is usually one in which the people understand what is going on and see how their support of sound community programs benefits their farming, their factories, their businesses, their schools, their churches, and their home life. Those in each social and economic grouping have learned that they can trust the other groupings; therefore, they do not let group loyalty interfere unduly with community morale.

7. Every community has a fund of experience in tackling local problems. The experiences people have had with community planning in the past will determine largely the degree to which they are willing to tackle co-operatively any problems troubling the community today.

8. Every community possesses a set of social values

to which the majority of people subscribe. Not long ago, a group of school teachers in a summer workshop represented six different communities. Each was asked to list those things which the people of his community considered most important. When these were put on the blackboard, the group was surprised to see the individuality which each community seemed to possess. There were a number of values, such as emphasis placed upon wealth or business success, which seemed to characterize every community to a certain degree; but there were some striking differences. In one community, importance was attached to getting through school, attaining a certain educational level, without much concern felt for the actual learning that took place. Another community, which was a suburban residential area and from which a high proportion of young people went to college, stressed actual learning and insisted upon fundamental education in its school system.

An introduction to developing a mature philosophy of community service, therefore, is an understanding of what is a community. It is more than an area, more than an economic center, for it is also a number of people sorted into various classes and groups, associated with each other in daily living. A community exists only because there are recognized common loyalties and shared social values. Its very richness holds the hope of the future.

QUESTION

2   *What Is the Basis of Community Life?*

I ONCE PLAYED second cornet in a military school band and derived great, even stirring, satisfaction from playing a march with the other members of the band. At times it seemed as though each player melted into a fusion of the whole, so that individual identities were lost and the group product afforded deep enjoyment to all. This feeling was driven home by contrast one wintry day when the cadet corps was holding its weekly review. The band had sounded off and supposedly was playing a march in front of the battalion. One by one the instruments froze, so that halfway down the field only the drums and the second cornet were playing—a solo performance, completely embarrassing at the time. Later, taken in perspective, this event has become a clearly remembered illustration of the tragicomic prima donna tendency in group action and a reminder of the richer satisfactions that come from activities shared with others.

For it is a truth constantly needing repetition that co-operation is the basis of community life. Yet it is also true that ours is a competitive age. American society is a competitive society, and much of its greatness is a result of competition. We value sports primarily because of their competitive nature; our grading system in school prepares for a competitive world. Competition even is found in law, medicine, and government service. There is competition between management and labor, deteriorating into conflict in the event of a strike or a lockout. But a society built on competition alone would eventually splinter. There must be, to check and balance, even more examples of co-operation which are less spectatcular but more pervasive, more enduring, more common as bread is common. Somehow or other in our American communities ways and means must be found of cushioning the divisive effects of extreme competition. Men's service clubs have led the way in this respect among business and professional men. But there are other areas of the social universe within which little communication and even less understanding exist. (See Guidepost 7.)

Civic leaders, therefore, should concentrate seriously upon stressing the importance of co-operation. To the extent that they compete in their daily work, to that extent should they support those co-operative efforts that seek to rebuild and counteract the effects of any competition carried to an extreme.

QUESTION
3   *How Should Knowledge Be Used?*

IN DEVELOPING our philosophy of community service, we must think through our attitude toward fact-finding as well as toward making use of specialists and experts. Often community workers get impatient at anyone trying to assess a situation objectively. They prefer to work on a hunch, rely on intuition, or just hope that things will break right. In their businesses or in building a home, they want the facts; they make use of facts. But when it comes to social engineering, they make light of serious attempts to get what might prove useful information.

But facts have to be interpreted; that is where broad

social experience is helpful. Facts together with experience tend to assure success. The same thing holds true for the mastery of techniques involved in community service. The use of techniques that alienate a large part of the community, or the pushing ahead with a campaign before adequate groundwork has been laid, shows an unwillingness to make enough use of the knowledge that is available. Even after we get all possible facts and after we have studied all of the proposed techniques, we still will have much improvisation to do. But the important thing is to let the facts take us as far as they will, let the techniques make our contribution as effective as possible, and we will increase the odds considerably in our favor.

QUESTION

4   *How Should We Look at Change?*

COMMUNITIES ARE changing constantly. Their geographic areas expand and contract, their populations rise and decline, and their economic and professional services ride the crests and troughs of the business cycle. The fluid area of social relationships—informal groups, clubs, and organizations; the institutions of the church, the school, the family, and government—is likewise subject to a bombardment of new and forceful stimuli. The mantle of leadership passes from one pair of shoulders to another, and community loyalty meets or fails the strains placed upon it.

What is significant is not the fact of change so much as the attitude community leaders take toward it. Some view it as a threat; others, as a promise of a better day ahead.

Just as there are persons who apply the brakes to the wheels of progress, so there are those who constantly seek to accelerate the speed of those wheels. They do this at times without much idea of the direction in which the wheels are moving. Their activity may occasionally serve a useful purpose if others are on hand to take advantage of the momentum they have generated and guide the vehicle of society toward a destination desired and needed by the community. But who are these agitators? They can be classed as crusader and campaigner.

1. The crusader puts a noble cause first. He exhorts and he pesters; he antagonizes and he enlists support; he forces people to take a stand for or against his cause before they have really formed a sound judgment; he seeks powerful allies and he has no fear of powerful foes. He lives in a world needing immediate, violent change; he is not concerned about the chain reaction his own change might set in motion, just as long as his cause is established, triumphant, and glorious. He often is selfless and possesses a nobility of spirit which far exceeds the breadth of his vision. When such leaders capture an organization or an institution and start on their crusade, the net effect of their efforts is determined finally by the social durability of their cause. If it can outlast the havoc wrought by its establishment, society judges it good and rewards its crusader with a place in the Hall of Fame. Unfortunately, many causes cannot stand the test of time, and the attempt to stir up social change proves to have been in vain.

2. The campaigner wants a job or an enhanced social position and is willing to enlist every sundry cause in his campaign. He need not be a seeker for political

office, either. Instead, he may be wanting to establish himself firmly in the business community, as a school administrator, an efficient clergyman, or an up-and-coming social worker. He probably does believe in the progress for which he is fighting, but he believes in himself even more. He, too, seeks social change, for as changes occur he is in position to climb the ladder of opportunity still higher. He may muckrake, cajole, or promise the world with a plywood fence around it; he may appeal to prejudice, to racial divisions, to religious differences, and thereby get the community worked into a state of high emotional excitement. He as an individual may procure what he wants, but he leaves to others the task of soothing ruffled feelings and putting the pieces of community back together again. No one can quite figure out exactly what goal he is trying to achieve for the community, but that is because of the smoke screen which he is careful to raise.

Crusading and campaigning do have a place in community life. Their shortcomings become apparent, however, when change just for the sake of change is the major emphasis. An angry beehive produces little honey, just as a community experiencing one emotional crisis after another finds it hard to settle down to the task of making life more pleasant and more abundant for all of its citizens.

Some men and women in positions of leadership and responsibility oppose social change as a matter of principle. They do this for a variety of motives; nor are they always consistent in the targets which they attack. We might classify such leaders as sentimentalist, cynic, and conservative.

1. Some prominent people in the community peri-

odically are overcome by waves of nostalgia. They think of the "good old days," make them the measure of progress or deterioration, and actively seek to forestall any further change in the community to which they feel so tightly bound. But, try as they will, sincerely and courageously, they cannot turn back the clock. In trying to do so, they can damage seriously the mechanism of the social organization which ticks along steadily and inevitably. Such leaders place their own sentimentality above a realistic appraisal of present community needs. Sentiment has a place, to be sure, in the community loyalty of every citizen, but it should not be the guiding element in that loyalty.

2. Every community has a few people, usually not in important positions of civic leadership, who take a defeatist attitude toward all efforts at community improvement. Somewhere in the past they got their own fingers burned while trying to help others pull their chestnuts out of the fire, so that altruism becomes for them a delusion and a snare. "You can't put over a program like that in this town. People don't want to do things differently," they frequently say. Or they discount the motives of someone unselfishly seeking the good of the community. Their plea would be, "Let things alone. Why bother? You only make matters worse." As long as such cynics are not newspaper editors, highly placed financiers, city officials, county judges, or others in authority, such opposition to social change is more amusing than vicious.

3. A third group opposing social change includes some of those at the top. Fortunately, in America it is no crime for a person to arrive at the top, to find himself in a favored position because of family background, by

dint of hard labor, by careful planning as well as by self-sacrifice. And since we live in a competitive age, those at the top know that there are a number of contenders for their position. Consequently, in the opinion of some of these, anything which preserves the status quo helps keep them at the top; anything that threatens it also threatens their personal position. So they oppose change, frequently quite openly and frankly, but at times indirectly and subtly. Sometimes, such leaders, following human inclinations to which we all are prone, prefer to perpetuate their own prestige, even though community welfare itself might suffer.

Not to be included among those resisting social change are those who ask intelligent, penetrating questions about projected programs. A doubting Thomas can be a community asset if his questioning is not so chronic that even worth-while projects are stymied.

The most successful community workers, and we can be one of these, will not resist change, nor will they purposely try to stir it up for the sake of a treasured cause or of personal advantage. Instead, they will seek to guide social change. For us, this means:

1. We will try to understand what major changes are already under way and will be able to select those that have community significance.

2. We will have social patience, because we realize that timing is all-important and that an impetuous approach to community problems accomplishes little in the long run.

3. We will realize that at one time some institution or organization can serve best as an agency for one type of social change, while for other types different organizations are better.

4. We will know that the role of the community leader is really that of expressing group and community sentiments as quickly as these take form and that this role is not that of domination or dictatorship or the unflagging adherence to our own pet preconceived ideas.

5. We will foresee as best we can the social consequences of strengthening some trend under way and use this foresight in helping the group or community work out its own welfare. (See Guidepost 6.)

QUESTION
5

*What Is Our Part
in Community Service?*

OUR PHILOSOPHY OF community service must include the part that we as individuals are to play in the process of social improvement. Each of us, at some time or other, finds himself charged with the role of leadership; more often we are cast as followers. Even though we may be chosen more often as leaders, we alternate between the spotlight of authority and the gentle glow of followership.

Let's look first at community leaders. Often we will find many people mentioned by others as community leaders who never think of themselves at all in that capacity. They admit that they help with this community program or that organizational task, but they concentrate so hard on getting a good job done that they never ask themselves what position of importance they may be attaining. When we analyze the reasons given for naming such people as leaders, we will ordinarily find these characteristics:

1. Such leaders believe in the democratic way. They

have faith in the ability of the people about them to reach decisions which make sense. They see an implicit goodness in human nature and call forth the best that is in those with whom they work.

2. Moreover, community leaders act in the democratic way. We doubtless can name several persons who have great faith in people but who have not yet mastered the techniques by which people are allowed to reach their own decisions. We as democratic leaders, as we take our responsibility seriously, will try to remember that people are more important than a program and that respect for personality should outweigh achievements gained at the cost of unnecessarily starting a conflagration of conflict. The democratic leader, because he recognizes his leadership as a trust and himself as a spokesman for the group he serves, knows that the opinion of many people on community problems is sounder than the judgment of a single egotist.

3. Such leaders take seriously the parable of the talents. To the extent that they have abilities to be enlisted in the common cause, they make use of those abilities. Where they have advantages of education, training, influence, and personal traits that inspire confidence, they willingly assume responsibilities in line with their talents.

But leaders cannot do everything. There is much chore-work to community efforts. This need not be drudgery, but there are innumerable details that someone must follow up. These details fit into a pattern seen by those charged with the general planning, but there must be much delegation of responsibility to community workers ready to serve in one small task after another. After all, walls are built one brick at a

time, and the small contributor has just as much right
to take pride in the completed task as the one who had
the lead. We as community workers, therefore, will
derive a satisfaction from our work for these reasons:

1. We see the importance of the small job well done.

2. We know that leaders, especially in community
programs where criticism may be great and financial
rewards even negative, need continued encouragement
and support.

3. We realize that the best training for enlarged leadership is the competent discharge of one task after another, so that a general perspective is gained.

4. We know that the shirking attitude of "let George
do it" is striking like a canker at the heart of American
national well-being and is crippling worthy efforts at
community improvement. In other words, we take
seriously our individual responsibility to make democracy vital in our own home town in the belief that it
will then be exportable by example to an ever-widening
area.

No wonder then that the American Council for the
Community has selected as a slogan part of the Oath of
the Athenian City-State which pledges, "we will trans-
mit this Community not only not less but greater and
more beautiful than it was transmitted to us."

And this community is our own home town.

PROCEDURES FOR CIVIC LEADERS: 20 GUIDEPOSTS

IT HAS BEEN a great temptation for me to make this handbook serve the same purpose as the *Book of Household Hints* which tells with clarity and by use of diagrams how to put in a stem washer to stop a steady trickle from a faucet. But with that type of book, helpful though it may be, we become at best a tinkerer. Indeed, our tinkering sometimes makes the plumber's bill much higher than it would have been, had we called him in the first place.

So it is with social relations. There is a complexity to them that makes oversimplification almost as great a danger as failure to enlighten at all. Nevertheless, there are some guideposts, some actual how-to-do-it's, which can be set forth by experienced authorities in community and group leadership. These suggested procedures take on added meaning in the light of the earlier sections of the book. Each person preparing one of the following guideposts has a special competence in the area about which he is writing. None of them claims infallibility, but each suggestion is well worth the trial.

1   *How to Find Community Specialists*

COMMUNITIES SHOULD avail themselves of every aid obtainable in the struggle to solve problems. It is wise to know every resource—local, state, and national—and to make the most intelligent application of it to local conditions.

I. *Why Communities Should Call on Specialists*

1. *It's Economical.* A community saves when its efforts are guided by those who know best. It saves in time. It saves in the energies of its people. It saves in dollars and cents when errors and wasted motions are avoided.

2. *It's Educational.* The presence on the scene of someone with a background of experience and training does more than help solve a specific problem. The expert will aid in the training of local people. He will bring in new ideas, widen horizons, and leave with the local people a new sense of the importance of facts and of the process of finding out.

3. *It's an Investment.* To have contact with an array of specialists is to build up a fund of resources. The future will be more secure when the leader knows that, come what may, he has an ace in the hole to call upon.

II. *Types of Specialists to Know About*

In this day and age specialization has become a

Guidepost 1 by John H. Given, Community Consultant, Lexington, Kentucky.

watchword, and the understanding of the complexities of community life has not escaped. Each of the many facets of community life has attracted the efforts of men who have accumulated a body of knowledge and know-how concerning it. The informed leader will have at least an acquaintanceship with the more important of these to call upon when the occasion demands.

1. The emphasis that the *sociologist* makes is upon social relationships, processes, and products. How is this community put together, how did it get that way, what are the human results? If your community's problem lies in this area, the sociologist will be interested and helpful.

Sometimes in this area the problems are weighted with a concern over attitudes, feelings, and prejudices. At this point the sociologist's twin, the *social psychologist*, is the one to call upon. More often than not, the two are the same person.

2. Ever since our modern world has decreed that it shall help those who cannot help themselves, men have been learning the most intelligent, efficient, and humane way of extending that help. The persons who represent this profession of enlightened helping are known as *social workers*. Theirs is the job of assisting all those who, if left to their own devices, would be unable to achieve a decent, satisfying way of life. (See Guidepost 12.)

Into the province of social work there fall all those problems which arise when a person or a group is disadvantaged by nature, nurture, or man, and if not assisted would fall by the wayside.

If your community, then, is burdened with homeless

children, aged blind, penniless widows, or under-privileged slum children, the tools and understandings of the social worker should be called upon.

3. The wisest use of land space, the best location for home and market, the allotment of room for play, and most efficient highway connections between all these are some of the more important concerns of the *city planner*. He has been assisted in his work by the *ecologist*, who is concerned with the interrelationships, in space, between peoples, industries, types of activities. The invasion of a section by a newcomer and the estimate of future population in an area are typical problems. Together these two can give assistance not only for correcting present conditions but more especially in the preparation of long-range city plans.

4. In searching for the most meaningful use of our increased free time, and for an improved educational tool, there has been developed a know-how in the constructive, creative use of leisure by the *recreation specialist*. No longer is it felt that needs are met by furnishing boys with a ball and bat or grown-ups with an occasional Chautauqua. It is now seen that all age groups need a well-balanced year-round program under trained leadership. If this is the problem before your town, the recreation specialist will be of invaluable assistance. (See Guidepost 14.)

5. It is not unusual to find a community in the doldrums. People may be listless, apathetic, or downright uninterested in conditions. Furthermore, local leaders may not be able to arouse their fellows. At this point it is often wisest to import an outsider with zeal and passion for social betterment. This *community evange-list*, being able to say much that the local leaders know

but can't say, may be able to stir the folks, act as a social irritant, and put the community on the march!

III. *Where Help Can Be Found*

Every community, regardless of size, has contact with someone representing the larger world. The agricultural extension worker, the Farm Bureau agent, the district Grange representative, the executive director of the Council for Social Planning, the minister, all have contact through their organizations with county, state, and national groups. Each of these will be glad to put a questioning citizen in touch with someone, who, if he cannot help, will know of someone else who can. Furthermore, most colleges and universities now have departments of sociology and social work and, in some instances, bureaus of community service. An appeal to these sources should route you to the one you need.

IV. *Cautions on the Use of Experts*

The misuse of an expert is in many ways more harmful than failure to use one at all. When he becomes a crutch for a person or group to lean upon, neither one matures or profits by the experience. When a person or group comes to view the problem only through the eyes of the expert and not in its community setting, then a distorted vision and disjointed action are the result.

The expert should be used within his field of specialization to the limit of his usefulness and no more. He should be called upon just as long as his presence applies and no more. He should be questioned and trusted on those factors about which he is informed but should not be invited to extend his prestige to other fields. We must remember that many problems cut across fields of interest, and the intelligent lay leader must balance and weigh and integrate the help of the several experts and hold to the main task. He must not allow the effort to be led astray by the persuasion of an expert in one field. The best guarantee for this desirable goal is sound help at the start, careful guidance, and the development of general perspective.

GUIDEPOST

2 *How to Map Communities*

SINCE NEIGHBORHOOD and community boundaries exist in the minds of the local people, it is necessary to confer with them and find out just where they think the boundary lines should be drawn on a map. First of all, however, you must have some clear idea of what area a community covers. Usually it will not correspond with such political units as the incorporated city, the precinct, or township. Nor will it in most cases be the same as a school district.

Here is a southern community.

The heavy lines show the neighborhoods, which are the local face-to-face groupings of the rural people. The community in this case is the cluster of those neighborhoods whose people look to the center for the satisfaction of their economic, recreational, and educational needs. Frequently rural people speak of their

Guidepost 2 by Douglas Ensminger, Ford Foundation, New Delhi, India.

neighborhood as their "community," but for many purposes it is useful to think of the *neighborhood* as the smaller area of from fifteen to thirty families, centered about some church, school, or crossroads store. The word community is thus reserved for the larger trade

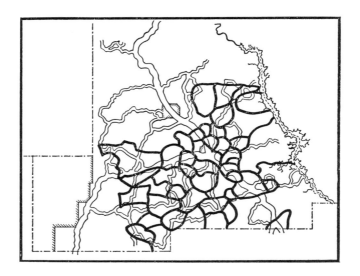

center community or a grouping of several neighborhoods which cluster about a town or village where there are a number of institutions and services.

The social importance of the *neighborhood groupings* varies somewhat from region to region. Where they exist they can be used as a sound basis for community organization.

Large metropolitan centers, like the one shown below, may seem a far cry from the smaller towns which comprise with their surrounding area the great majority of American communities.

Such large collections of hundreds of thousands, at times millions of people, can act as a total unit in some affairs. For example, residents of Pittsburgh and Allegheny County, Pennsylvania, who did much to reduce the smoke nuisance which had plagued that city, succeeded only through a large-scale effort. Yet

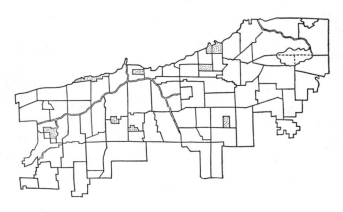

Pittsburgh, like all metropolitan areas, consists of a number of communities, most of them with special names and with ability to act corporately about any problem of common concern. These communities, although well within the metropolitan area, have their own complement of civic clubs, churches, schools, businesses, and fire and police protection.

If communities, then, are so varied, how do we locate and delineate them? Before starting out, be sure to consult the Agricultural Extension Service at your state university for any community map that they might possess, since in many states the rural sociologists have already done considerable mapping. But if you decide to do the job yourself you can either go out into the community and visit people in widely scattered locations or else ask a representative group to come together into the urban center for a meeting at which you get their help in drawing tentative neighborhood and community boundaries.

I. Visiting people in each local area

1. If you visit rural people living in each local area, take with you a highway map showing roads, villages, schools, churches, rural dwellings, and other landmarks. The more detailed the map, the easier it will be for the people to locate the neighborhood boundaries.

2. Ask each person interviewed, "What is your neighborhood called?" "How far does your neighborhood extend down this road?" or "Where does the last family considered to be a member of the neighborhood live in this direction?" Do this for each road, marking an "X" beyond the last family belonging to the neighborhood. Then connect the "X's" with a line and the neighborhood area is mapped.

3. Having mapped the neighborhood then ask your informant, "What large center do the people of this neighborhood visit most frequently? What other neighborhoods associate with your neighborhood? What do you share and have in common with other neighborhoods?" This gives you the basis for knowing which neighborhoods are grouped together in one community. Generally it is a good idea to talk to at least two persons in each neighborhood before inking in the neighborhoods and community boundaries on a county map.

II. Inviting local people to a county meeting

If you are pressed for time, you may develop tentative neighborhood and community boundaries by inviting local people to a county meeting. If you follow this procedure, be sure to invite people from all sections of the county. At the meeting have the group gather around the highway map and locate all the areas having a known name. Indicate the trade or possible community centers. The group should then draw in tentative neighborhood and community boundaries. At an early date the map should be corrected by local people who can be called together in each community.

III. Where neighborhoods are unimportant

In areas where neighborhoods are weak or nonexistent you will be able to approximate community boundaries if a number of businessmen from the town or village center locate on a highway map the most distant families (which come into the center regularly to trade), on each road radiating from the center. By consulting a number of people you can get a combined judgment, indicating the approximate community boundaries. If you are not sure where the lines dividing communities should be drawn, talk to the people in the in-between areas to find out where their loyalty lies.

GUIDEPOST
3

*How to Get
the Facts about the Community*

EACH FACT WHICH you collect about some single part of the economy of your community is only meaningful as it fits into the picture puzzle of

Guidepost 3 by Helen Bridgman Fritz, formerly management adviser in Community Activities and Tenant Relations, Chicago Housing Authority.

people's everyday working and consuming. There are many complicated ways which have been worked out to collect and record statistics for economic analysis, but undertaking these takes a lot of time and money. It is best to keep your task as simple as possible. The purpose here is to suggest a few basic points for departure which will help you fit together the facts about your community's economic life.

I. Employment

1. Where does the income in your community come from? The latest population census, Series III, lists income of people in your county by major source. You will be able to tell from these figures what proportion of the people in your town earn their living in agriculture, by industry, from tourists, etc. Most communities have some one function around which other parts of their economic life revolve. Knowing what that aspect is and how important it is in your community's living will be helpful in planning programs for its improvement.

2. How many people are out of jobs? What kinds of work would they do if they were working? What proportion of the married women in your town must work to supplement family income? The State Employment Service can supply you with recent figures for your town and your county as well as for your state. What happens to the employment pattern within a year (seasonal changes) and over a period of ten years (cyclical changes in the nation) will be a guide in determining the economic stability of your community as compared to other towns in your state.

II. Population Trends

Are people moving to or away from your town? In what age groups does migration seem to be taking place most rapidly? What is the present proportion of productive workers to dependents (people between 15 and 60, or those who work, and the rest of the population) on the basis of the last census? When you discover trends, ask yourself what seems to cause these. They are a good indication of the economic opportunity in your community.

Agriculture, business, and industry are three areas of economic living for which you want to collect more specific facts. The questions at the end of each section are there to help you fit these facts together and make the most useful sense out of them.

III. Basic Facts about Agriculture

By finding out the size, the value and ownership of farms, farm income and expenditures you will have the story of farm prosperity and how the farmers are using it. These facts are all in Series I and II of the Census of Agriculture, which is taken every five years by the Department of Agriculture. Your local county agent can help you get a copy of the most recent census of your county and make the charts to set down the facts you need. Compare the most recent census with several preceding it and then compare the changes in your community with those in selected surrounding counties and in the state as a whole. You may discover that farmers in your county have increased their incomes but not so rapidly as have people who farm in other parts of the state. Write the county agent in those counties to find out what the reasons are. Maybe you will think of several yourself.

Questions to keep in mind as you study the facts about agriculture in your county:

1. Would markets be more accessible if transportation facilities were improved?

2. Are local credit sources aware of the possibilities of good farm investments?

3. Do they make advantageous loans to farmers?

4. Do farmers have access to the best information about productivity and crops, and are they using their land to best advantage?

5. Is cheap power available so that farmers can increase labor-saving devices on their farms?

6. Do farmers know about the governmental agricultural agencies in the county?

7. Are local farm products used by the local business and industrial concerns of your community in every way possible?

IV. Business in Your Town

The retail sales in your community depend on the number of neighborhoods which use your town as a shopping center and the amount of money those people who patronize your town's business spend there.

By figuring out the retail sales per person in your town and in nearby towns of similar size you can measure how well your town is meeting the shopping needs of people in the vicinity. The latest Census of Manufacture, put out by the Census Bureau in Washington, includes figures on the total retail sales as well as the sales totals on a number of different goods and services for each incorporated area. It may be that your local chamber of commerce or one of the civic clubs has worked out more recent figures which would give you a truer picture of the present situation. By dividing the town population by these figures you arrive at the per capita sales on each item. Do the same for the other communities you have selected and you will have a basis for comparison. (See Guidepost 2 for relationship between trade area and community boundaries.)

Questions to consider in studying your facts on retail trade:

1. For what goods and sources do the people in your community have to travel to other areas? List them. Compare the per capita sales on different items (like furniture, farm equipment, clothing, groceries) with those in the towns around yours.

2. Are there local farm markets which bring farmers to town?

3. Is there a friendly feeling between town and country people? Is there a tendency for farmers to feel that town people consider themselves superior? Do the business, civic, and church groups in town encourage town-country understanding in any way?

4. Are adequate parking, recreation, and resting places provided for people who come to town?

V. *Manufacturing and Industry*

Many small towns have increased their general economic level by bringing in small industrial firms. They have found that the presence of an up-to-date manufacturing plant is an asset not only as a means of increasing income but because it lends variety and thus greater stability to the community's whole economic activity.

Industry is becoming an increasingly important influence in the economic life of small towns. It is important to find out the number of people employed, their wage scales, and the conditions of work in industries already located in your town. The manager of each plant will be able to supply you with this information. Compare these facts with established working conditions and wages in other nearby factories.

If your town has unions, what are their relations with management and what is the town's attitude toward them? It is often possible to see what interest the various managements have in your community as a whole by seeing what their attitudes are to its workers. Likewise, it is useful to find out whether the unions have an opportunity to participate in the welfare of the community.

VI. *Prospective Industrial Expansion*

Local income can be increased as the value of local manufactured products is raised. However, in an economy as competitive as our own, it is only profitable if as many available resources as possible are used advantageously.

The following points should be kept in mind as you think about possible new industry for your town:

1. Do you have an inventory of the natural resources in the region? The State Department of Mines will be able to help you on this.

2. Do you know your town's available labor supply? You have some data on this already, but you may want to get additional information as well. Many small towns are making labor surveys to find out exactly how many people there are, and what kinds of work they

are able to do. The Bureau of Labor Statistics in Washington can help you get this data.

3. Transportation, as has already been pointed out, is vital to progress in any town. Do you have a map showing roads, railroads, bus, and river transportation facilities?

4. Power availability must be assessed, too. Find out what are the local sources for power and what the present power capacity is.

With these data, you should be able to determine what kinds of industries would best fit into the economic pattern of your community.

In the last few years many state-wide agencies as well as organizations with nation-wide scope have been set up to help communities develop their industry on a sound basis. The U. S. Department of Commerce, Washington, now collects a number of different indices on economic life in small cities and will make this information available to you if you write them about it. Many states have publicly supported agencies (such as planning or agricultural and industrial development boards) whose whole purpose is to study the best ways in which communities could develop their agriculture and industry. Practically all states have chambers of commerce working on their problems of economic expansion. In a few states the universities are now offering their resources to help local and state-wide groups study their economic activity and development. Your state may have these and other agencies ready to work with you on your community's needs.

This outline is only meant to point the way. The rest is up to you and your community. Nearly every community has unrealized opportunities for development and improvement, but it takes interest, imagination, and hard work to find them. It will probably not be some one big project but a number of small ones which will make the most positive long-run differences to your whole community. If the people in your town and in the surrounding neighborhoods pull together, everyone's chances for a good living can be increased.

4   *How to Use Community Surveys*

THERE IS MOST certainly no one best way of going about gathering the facts needed as a basis for community planning and action. The method to be used must depend upon a great variety of different factors. These include the area of concern about which the facts are to be gathered, the experience and skills of the persons involved in the process, the time and personnel available, the amount and kind of information that has already been gathered, and the ways in which the facts are to be used. The following is a brief description of some of the various ways of fact-gathering that have proven effective in different situations.

I. Research Studies

Research studies are *primarily concerned with the development of a scientific body of knowledge* in the field under investigation. Because of their intensive nature they must usually be confined to a limited field.

Guidepost 4 by A. F. Wileden, Professor of Rural Sociology, University of Wisconsin.

Furthermore, the work should be done by trained research analysts. Entire books have been written, and entire courses are given, dealing with research method, and it would be out of place to elaborate on it here. It must suffice to say that there are rather definite steps or procedures which a research study should follow.

It is doubtful if a scientific research study is a preferred method to use if an action program in the community is the immediately desired objective. Because of their nature, research studies are usually made without any thought of the immediate application of findings. As a matter of fact, the discipline of an action program might possibly interfere with the much desired scientific validity of such a research study.

II. Co-operative Surveys

It is at the point where research studies are weak that co-operative surveys are strong. They *involve the co-operation of the "surveyed"* and thereby include them in the fact-finding enterprise. There are all degrees of co-operation, of course. On the one hand, the local co-operation may be little other than permitting the use of names of respected local people on a sponsoring committee. On the other hand, local people may carry the complete responsibility for planning, conducting, and reporting the findings of the survey with outside personnel serving only as a technical survey consultant. The more preferred procedure is to operate somewhere between these two extremes.

The idea of the co-operative survey is based upon about three principles: (1) that true advancement depends upon a knowledge of conditions; (2) that learning starts with the familiar, the near-at-hand, the experienced; (3) that facts have more interest and motivating power when you gather them yourself. These three principles make the co-operative survey a valuable technique in the field of community organization.

Similar to the research study, the co-operative survey must go through rather definite stages of development. You will notice that they correspond in many respects to the general discussion of fact-finding on pages 32-39. These stages may be about as follows:

1. Agreement as to the problem (or problems) to be studied.

2. Setting up the organization and securing the needed personnel to carry on the study.

3. Development of the plans and questionnaires needed to gather the desired information.

4. Gathering the desired information in both the field and from sources already available. This may involve some training for the people who gather the data.

5. Classification and tabulation of the data gathered in the field and from secondary sources. Again, this may involve some training for the people who are to do the tabulating.

6. Interpreting and presenting the findings, both in written reports and directly to the people in the area under study.

7. Evolving plans based on these findings for dealing with the problems under study.

8. Putting these plans into action.

The importance of securing the services of a competent technical consultant to advise and help with the survey cannot be overestimated. The assistance of such a consultant is needed to help with the planning of the survey. They can give valuable assistance with the preparation of questionnaires to be used, with the training of the people who are to gather the data, with the supervision of the tabulations, and with the preparation of reports. Sociologists are often called upon to serve in this capacity.

III. Self-Appraisal and Analysis

Frequently a community requires a rather systematic picture of itself and its needs, but lacks either the time or the desire to undertake a more elaborate type of community survey. Or a survey may have been made in recent years, and only a quick appraisal is needed to bring the information up to date. Under such circumstances it is desirable that some *less time consuming method* be used to appraise the situation before the development of plans and undertaking of action programs. As a matter of fact, such methods of fact-finding are probably desirable in more situations than is practically possible through the use of research studies or co-operative surveys. Such methods include the use of community score cards, community check sheets, or the setting up of appraisal committees.

1. *Community Score Cards.* The basic idea back of the community score card is to set up a standard against which a community can be scored or ranked. Such score cards are used in many fields, and community score cards have been used in various parts of this country for many years. West Virginia, for example, used a state-wide system of community scoring starting as early as 1917. During the next seventeen years 350 communities were scored, some as many as fifteen times. Different types of score cards were used for different

types of communities, and the score cards were changed from time to time. However, they always included attention to the different phases of community life. Any professional worker is in position to supply interested persons with samples of different types of score cards.

2. *Community Check Sheets.* Some community score cards can properly and probably even more appropriately be used as community check sheets. However, sometimes these check sheets need to be simpler than these score cards, and need to be adapted to varying community situations. These are situations, for example, where a mutual recognition of local problems is essential. A committee of local people may easily work out such a check sheet to meet these conditions, including only those items which they believe may apply. This list might then be checked by a cross section of the people in the community.

Such a check sheet may also provide opportunity to express the desirability of working toward the solution of one problem rather than another. This expression of the attitude of the people of the community is as helpful in determining programs for action as the recognition of the problems themselves. Sometimes, also, the two are quite different.

The following is a suggested type of community problem check sheet which a committee might use as a starter. It includes both opportunity to indicate the problems and expression of the desirability of attempting their solution.

CHECK SHEET OF PROBLEMS IN THE .... COMMUNITY

Check in the first column those problems that you believe are the most serious, and in the second column those you believe the community can and should do something about.

Community Problems	Which five are the most serious. (check)	Which can and should the community do something about (check)
Churches not work together		
Dissension in the community		
Inadequate fire protection		
Inadequate health services		
Inadequate housing		
Lack of employment opportunities		
Lack of zoning regulations		
Lack of understanding between different groups in the community		
Laws not properly enforced		
Need better merchandising methods		
Need for better relations between farm and nonfarm people		
Need for youth clubs		
No buildings for community use		
No plans for war emergency		
Not enough organizations of the proper kind		
Poor conservation methods		
Poor schools		
Poor streets or highways		
Schools not conscious of responsibility to the community		
Too many farmers follow poor farming practices		
Too many organizations		
Unattractive physical surroundings		
Unsanitary conditions		
Youth delinquency		

3. *Evaluation Committees.* If a program has been going on for some time, and a self-appraisal is desirable, an evaluation committee is an effective way to go about it. It is easy for a community that has been successful in its undertakings to get into the habit of doing only certain things and neglecting other equally important things. Or a community may be emphasizing only certain ways of doing things that they have found effective to the extent that they have become traditional with them, while other equally good ways may be neglected. In these more successful and experienced communities an evaluation committee should be not only a valuable means of fact-finding, but might also well concern itself with evaluation of on-going programs. Objective introspection by members of the committee is equally as important as any of the other methods of fact-finding suggested herein.

However, objective evaluation can only result when the personnel of the committee are carefully chosen and when they are given complete freedom to make the necessary inquiries and to express themselves. Such a committee should therefore include in its membership as many people in the community who are not active in the program under consideration as are active in it. Some might well even be constructively critical. It should include people who represent different points of view in the community. It should also include, probably best serving as consultants, professional people working in the fields under consideration. Also it should include, probably also best serving as a consultant, a competent professional person in the field of group methods and community organization.

IV. *Mass Interviews*

Another general method of fact-gathering which has frequently been ignored is what we might well call the mass interview. *Gathering facts in a group situation* takes less time than some other methods, and it is possible to cover a broad area of inquiry. It also has the definite advantage of getting at the interaction of people in a group situation. People speak differently and usually more accurately in the presence of others than when they are being interviewed as individuals. Furthermore, differences of opinion are revealed in a way that it is difficult to discover on a person-to-person basis.

However, there are also limitations in the mass interview. Frequently many things are not revealed that would be reported without hesitation in a personal interview. You usually get only the matter of fact or favorable side of the picture, and certain personal factors are not revealed at all. This makes it essential to follow up the mass interview with other forms of fact-gathering.

V. *Descriptive Statements*

What we might call the descriptive statement is another valuable method of discovering and presenting facts about a community. It may be *prepared by a resident of the community,* or *by the so-called "participant observer."*

Even descriptive statements prepared by local people may take different forms. Local high school students in Social Science or English classes may be asked to write papers or themes on such topics as

"What My Community Needs Most" or "What I Like Best About My Community." Or a resident of the community may be motivated to write a history of the community and its people. Many interesting novels are produced in this way, and at the same time are factually accurate.

The participant observer, particularly the trained observer, if he can live in the community for a period of time, can often make a distinctive contribution to understanding the life of the community. As a matter of fact, it is often possible for such a trained observer to secure an understanding of the people and of the group processes in the community that can be gathered in no other way.

VI. Secondary Sources

Much information has already been gathered and is already available about most communities. Anyone making a community survey can well *start with this secondary source material which is already available.* It will undoubtedly need supplementing and bringing up to date.

GUIDEPOST
5

How to List
the Community's Organizations

SOCIAL SCIENTISTS generally refer to clubs and associations as formal groups. A "formal group," as used in this book, is one with a name, some officers or recognized leaders, and a fairly regular place

Guidepost 5 by Irwin T. Sanders.

and time of meeting. Every group worker will want to get the general picture of the group life in the community so that the particular place of his own organization can be more easily understood. Learning more about other groups may give him some ideas for making his own leadership more helpful. Here are some of the things to learn about the formal groups of the community.

I. The Kind of Information Needed

For each organization, write down its name, its purpose and activities, the membership it serves, the outstanding leaders. This is a large order but is a task to be divided up among several people interested in knowing more about their community. In some communities, where organizational competition is most pronounced, the number of formal groups would total from 55 to 75. But where there is such complexity there is even more need for a careful analysis of the organizational pattern.

Such a survey would show what areas of life and what community needs are not being met by any existing group. These needs have been listed by one writer as (1) *the God need,* or spiritual, religious, ethical; (2) *the Job need,* or the economic wants of food, clothing, and shelter; (3) *the Fun need,* or recreation, entertainment, esthetic; (4) *the Health need;* and (5) *the Law need,* or order, which becomes less important as greater stress is placed on the God need. One of the basic principles of community organization is this: people must have a *sense of need* before they are willing to organize for and work hard on any community program. Launching a program before the need is felt locally is like jumping the gun; one has to come back to the starting point again.

The survey described here would also reveal what groupings (men and women, those of different economic levels, farm and city, race and nationality divisions) are being served adequately by existing organizations and what groupings are being neglected. Quite often some organizations are wholly expressions of one group and render important services to that group. For example, in a New England community only the Portuguese-Americans belong to St. Anthony's Social Club.

With such information before him, the officer of a group knows how to do a better job with his members. An outsider, with a program to get across to the people, could tell from such a survey whether the program he had in mind would best be served by working through some existing organization or organizations. Just because he has a new program or is interested in solving some community problem is no particular reason why he will have to start a new club or organization. Many active organizations with energetic leaders are constantly on the lookout for some worth-while activity to sponsor. An organization that has prestige in the community and is representative of the type of people for whom the program has been prepared might serve very well.

But whatever he decides to do, a knowledge of the existing organizations in the community gives any worker a headstart on those who see the community through a keyhole as it were, or merely in terms of some specialized interest which ignores all the organizational effort about them.

II. *A Form to Follow*

This is a form to use in making the organizational analysis just described above.

Be sure to gain the help of qualified people before beginning the survey.

Agree thoroughly ahead of time as to the method to be followed.

Include each and every organization which can be located in the community.

LISTING

		Organization A	Organization B	Organization C	Organization D
1. Name					
2. Purpose					
3. Chief Activities	1. 2. 3. 4.				
4. No. active members					
5. Type of member	:a. Sex :b. Age :c. Econ.[1] :d. Other[2]				
6. Regular meeting time					
7. Average attendance					
8. Organizations with which it co-operates	1. 2. 3. 4.				
9. Outstanding leaders	1. 2. 3. 4.				
10. Other Notes[3] of interest					

[1] Economic and occupational groupings such as landlords, tenants, businessmen, various income groups (under $1,000, $1,000-2,000, $2,000-3,000, over $3,000), farm or town.

[2] Other—would include such membership restrictions as religion, race, military service, prominent ancestors, etc.

[3] Other notes might include such factors as the name of organizations in conflict with the one being studied, a general observation about the vitality of the group, attitude of outsiders toward the group, and the attitude of group members toward the community, etc.

ANALYSIS

(Numbers correspond to items on list above)

1. The total number of organizations discovered: an actual count.
2. Which organizations have similar purposes?
   Which organizations have antagonistic purposes?
3. Which organizations carry on similar activities?
   What activities needed in the community are not being carried out by any organization?
   Which organizations no longer follow their original purpose?
4. What is the average size (in terms of members) of the community organization?
5. What important segments of the community are not being served by organizations?
6. What organizations meet at the same time?
   What days are most free of organizational meetings?
7. How well do people of the community attend meetings?
   Do certain groups attend more regularly than others?
8. What organizations are in co-operative relationships?
   Which organizations co-operate with no other organizations?
9. What leaders are influential in two or more organizations?
   Which of these are considered community as well as organizational leaders?
10. What general observations do the people who helped in the survey feel that they can agree upon?

How to Size Up
Changes in the Community

THE ALERT COMMUNITY leader will do well to remember that change is nearly always taking place and that it is his responsibility and opportunity to note what the new developments are, to know how they have come about, and to understand what they mean to the organized life of the community. He may want to see what contribution his organization can make toward determining the direction and rate of change; most assuredly he will want to assist the local people in their adjustment to new conditions.

I. Changes That Are Significant

Some changes affect organizations and communities more than others. Among the most important are:

1. Shifts in the population and facts about the people who are moving in or moving out of the community, their age, sex, skills, family organization, ethnic backgrounds, etc.

2. Changes in the way the people make their living through the introduction of new industries or new machinery, the development of new sources of power, the loss of markets, the availability of nonfarm employment, and the like.

3. Changes in the work habits of self-employed people and of hired workers in response to new patterns of employment in urban industries and in farming areas.

Guidepost 6 by Arthur Raper, Mutual Security Agency.

4. Changes in family incomes and in habits of spending as related to levels of living, use of medical and dental services, support of local organizations and activities, and so on.

5. Changes in availability of community services as affected by population shifts, occupational changes, and local economic conditions.

6. Changes in the thinking and loyalties of the people and in their attitudes toward organizational activities in response to changing conditions.

II. Finding Out How Changes Are Occurring

The primary thing that the community worker will need to keep in mind is that salient facts about the changes that are taking place are common knowledge of individuals here and there throughout the communities. He will need to accumulate these facts and have them available for such use as he and his organization may want to make of them.

If the community worker is an outsider, he will first of all need to find out what the local organizational leader already knows: namely, to whom to go for the special information wanted about the changes which are occurring.

By way of illustration, we will list here certain people whom the worker should see if he wishes to find out what changes are occurring in the spending habits of the people:

1. The grocers and department store merchants—for changes that have occurred in expenditures for food, clothing, and general household supplies of farm families and of urban families.

2. Furniture dealers and undertakers—for any appreciable changes in purchases of household equipment or in prices which families are willing to pay for funerals.

3. Hardware merchants, machinery salesmen, automobile dealers, and repairmen—for changes in expenditures for farm equipment, automobile maintenance, and so on.

4. Jewelers, barbers, and beauticians—for changes in their businesses.

5. The ticket agents at the railroad and bus stations—for changes in the travel habits of local people.

6. Local institutional leaders—for determining whether expenses for recreation, education, support of the church, and the like are on the increase or decrease.

7. Doctors, merchants, and landlords—for general facts about the payment of personal obligations.

8. The local banker—for changes in the amounts of money the people have on deposit and in savings accounts, and also their borrowings and repayments.

9. The local representative of the Production Credit Association and the Farmers Home Administration—for relative repayment of loans and prospective lendings.

10. The local representative of the Federal Land Bank—to determine whether maturities are being met when due, or if money is being deposited for future payments.

11. The county tax collector—for facts about the promptness of the payment of taxes by various segments of the population and whether tax delinquencies are piling up or being paid off.

12. Local real estate dealers—for information about changes in city and farm prices and volume of sales.

13. The county clerk's office—for records of real estate transfers, by types.

14. Life insurance and bond salesmen—for the status of their urban and rural patronage.

15. General community leaders—for the basic explanations of the reason back of any changes that have occurred.

III. Interpreting Community Change Through the Programs of Local Organizations

Some organizations will find their greatest usefulness in helping their members to interpret changing conditions and to meet them adequately. The program of any organization will need to be adjusted as changes occur. It will readily be seen that population shifts, for example, are related to the size and program of any particular organization. Changed ways of thinking among the local people may have profound effects on local organizational activities. Sometimes in response to such changes an old organization may well be disbanded, or a new one set up.

Life is dynamic. Organizations can render their greatest service only when the local leaders keep their program constructively adjusted to *current* conditions, which of course always include the latest changes that affect the life of the people in the local community.

GUIDEPOST

7   How to Deal with Local Conflict

SINCE IT IS unlikely that a community which has existed for any considerable length of time

Guidepost 7 by Edgar A. Schuler, Head, Department of Sociology, Wayne University.

would have enjoyed only completely harmonious and co-operative relationships, it is quite desirable for the would-be worker to have a navigator's chart which will show him where the reefs and submerged rocks of conflict are located, so that he may plot his course with safety.

I. The Importance of Understanding Local Conflict

1. *Recognized conflict.* Conflict which is actually going on in the local community may make it impossible for the community worker to carry out his assignment. Naturally this will depend upon how intense the conflict is and how widely the members of the community are affected.

2. *Undercover conflict.* If the conflict is kept largely under cover; that is, if it is actually going on but not openly, it may result in a nullification of the worker's efforts even after he has invested considerable time, energy, and ingenuity in getting a program under way. If the conflict is simply concealed from public view, there is always the possibility that it may break out into the open and disrupt many of the existing patterns of co-operation or organized activity within the community.

3. *The aftermath of conflict.* If the conflict has previously existed in the community but has been brought to an end, it is important for the worker to understand the type of adjustment, or what the sociologist calls "accommodation," which has been worked out. For example, the community worker should know whether the losing side in the recently ended conflict has fully accepted the status of loser and all that it implies, or whether there is external submission but internal or subjective refusal to accept the status of loser. If the

latter situation exists, the conflict only appears to have been ended, and it may be resumed whenever the dissatisfied loser feels strong enough again to end the truce and continue the fight. The uninformed worker may unintentionally add his weight to one side or the other of the scales and, without his wishing to, may precipitate what amounts to a continuation of the conflict.

II. What Types of Conflict Are Most Important to the Community Worker?

Three types of conflict of great significance to the community worker are farm versus nonfarm, social class, and organizational.

1. *Farm versus nonfarm conflict* is a widespread and persisting type of difficulty which seems to be inherent in the different types of activity performed by the farmer and the person who lives in the village or town but performs various service functions for the farmer. There seems to be real difficulty in avoiding misunderstanding between people who play these two occupational roles. The same thing holds true in general for labor and management.

2. *Class and caste conflict.* To the extent that the people of a community are organized into classes or castes, such social stratification seems to carry with it the possibilities of cleavages and hostility. Fear of the outbreak of such conflict, for example, may lead some members of the dominant classes in a given area to resort to repressive measures, even involving violation of the civil liberties of lower-class people.

3. *Organizational conflict.* Various forms of organizational conflict may be of importance in a given community. A number of these are illustrated.

(a) Family or kinship group conflicts: Feuding represents an extreme of one type, but strife within the larger kinship groups may be no less serious and significant even though the parties to the conflict are represented by decorous lawyers who resort only to verbal violence in waging their legalistic warfare.

(b) Political or governmental rivalries: The struggle to secure or to retain the seat of local government, symbolized by the location of the courthouse or county seat, is typical of this form.

(c) Educational disputes: Hostility may become intense in connection with conflicting ideas about the desirability of organizing a consolidated school, or of building a new schoolhouse—its location, major architectural features, and so on.

(d) Sectarian strife: Religious organizations sometimes develop an internal factionalism which splits up the entire community and may be as significant as conflict between denominations.

(e) Recreational conflict: Differing conceptions of what constitute the acceptable and desirable in play activities also may lead to conflict. Examples of this form of institutional conflict occur in connection with such local issues as whether or not to permit Sunday movies, public dance halls, pool halls, saloons, "juke joints," and so on.

(f) Mixed organizational conflicts: The preceding examples of conflict have dealt only with cases in which the organizations involved belonged to the same broad institutional type. It should be pointed out, however, that conflicts commonly occur between organizations of different institutional types. For example, differences may arise between the leaders or membership of an educational group, such as the Parent-Teacher Association, and of a primarily economic group, such as a farmers' organization; or between the athletic program of a high school and the weekday program of a church, over time and place of meeting. Such differences, minor at the beginning, may develop into bitter and far-reaching controversy.

III. What Should the Worker Do About Local Conflict?

1. *Understand it.* First of all, he should understand it. That is, (a) the worker needs to have a clear idea, first, of the groups or classes of people who were or are involved in the conflict. (b) He needs to know the basic causes of the conflict. In other words, he should understand what interests or motives make the conflict inevitable. (c) If the conflict has taken place in the past, what sort of readjustment has grown out of it? How have group relationships been changed as a result of the conflict situation?

2. *Steer clear of it, if possible.* On the basis of his understanding of the conflict it is obvious that the worker, if his assignment permits, should steer clear of any behavior which would tend to renew the conflict if it is past, or avoid his becoming identified with one or the other of the parties to a continuing conflict.

3. *If it interferes, reconcile it.* If the nature of the job to be done by the community worker requires community-wide participation, his understanding of the conflict should enable him to be circumspect and still sincere and independent in his relationships; consequently, he may incidentally help to heal the wounds caused by the conflict, rather than to inflame them.

4. *Build bridges.* To the extent that a proper fulfillment of his responsibilities calls for general co-operative activity, it may be necessary for him first to build bridges between the groups of people who have been divided by a social chasm before he can do anything really constructive in the way of organizational activity. Usually there will be some broader common purposes, or larger loyalties, which can be emphasized as the basis for co-operative activity.

5. *Work through local peacemakers.* If the basis of the conflict appears to be a clash of personalities rather than a deeply rooted opposition of interest, it should be possible to work through the conciliating, or peacemaker, type of personality which practically always is represented by at least a few capable persons in the community. Such individuals may provide the required detailed information, guidance, and help in developing a bridge of contacts which will close the gap separating the factions. For example, if it can be arranged to get representatives of the factions to have a meal, go on a fishing trip, or attend an out-of-town conference together and in the company of a conciliatory person, the foundation may be laid on which the bridge of good will may be built.

6. *Conflict-solving is not the main job.* Only one point further need be mentioned. It is not the responsibility of the worker to go out of his way to solve every conflict situation about which he may learn. Rather his responsibility in connection both with the conflict and with its resolution is determined by the organizational objectives which he has in mind or which are assigned to him.

*How to Organize Communities
Composed of Various Cultural Groups*

DIFFICULT ORGANIZATIONAL problems are encountered in communities which include diverse nationality groups. In such communities language, cultural, and religious barriers may segregate a large block of the people from the rest of the population. All too frequently the minority groups are neglected or even forgotten in community-wide programs. Sometimes their support is alienated from programs by failure to recognize their cultural values; at other times their support is not gained because the organizational adjustments necessary to reach them are not made. Minority groups may be an important part of your community, and you may find that they play a decided role in its functional organization. If you do not include them in your program, you may be overlooking a force which will be a decisive factor in the success of your program.

I. Use the Cultural Values of All the Groups

1. *Find out what nationality groups there are.* Ask the social welfare people, the health authorities, the politicians, labor organizations, and other people whose work brings them in contact with all sorts of people. Check the list of churches and other organizations for leads; e.g., a Swedish Lutheran church would indicate the presence of people of Swedish descent.

2. *Find out the cultural values of each group.* Talk to the social workers, health authorities, labor leaders, and other organizations having contacts with the vari-

Guidepost 8 by Earl H. Bell, Chairman, Department of Sociology and Anthropology, Syracuse University.

ous groups. Encourage them to tell you of their own and the experiences of others with people. Try to get information concerning

(a) religious beliefs, especially those that mark differences;

(b) family organization, particularly the lines of authority and responsibility;

(c) how they work together;

(d) their economic practices, especially desired possessions and avoided expenses;

(e) issues that lead to conflict with other groups;

(f) issues of conflict between the group and their children.

3. *Interpret your program in terms of their culture values.* Examine your program. Which of the values held by each group will it support? Perhaps all groups have a common value which will be supported by your program. But perhaps it will fit into the value systems of some groups differently than others. Then you will want to interpret your program in ways that each group appreciates. This does not mean that you should be dishonest. In fact you must be scrupulously careful to avoid such appearances. Perhaps your program may be related to one of their national heroes. If so, you have an excellent cue for its presentation to them.

4. *Meeting arrangements.* Be sure meeting arrangements do not run counter to the cultural values of *any* group.

(a) Time—The culture beliefs or customs of some groups may prevent their attending meetings on Sundays, and others on Saturdays or special holidays. Don't set the meeting for a date that will not permit the participation of some groups.

(b) Place of meeting—Similarly, beliefs and customs

of some groups may prevent them from attending a meeting in some places. The Amish group would not—in fact, could not—bring itself to go to a meeting in a theater.

(c) Ceremonies and formalities—Be careful that no formalities or ceremonies will offend any group. Even some Christian groups would be alienated by the use of the cross in a ceremony.

(d) Food—Many cultural groups have food taboos. If it seems desirable to have a luncheon meeting, be sure that the menu does not embarrass members of any of the groups attending.

(e) Entertainment—In meetings attended by several cultural groups it is best to stick to business. If you connect entertainment features with your meeting, be sure they are of a kind that will not offend any groups. In a community composed of old American stock and a German Mennonite group a joint meeting was held to discuss a community-wide program. Before discussing the program, the American group put on a short skit. This alienated the support of the German Mennonites who condemn all kinds of make-believe. They never attended another meeting. Even if none of the groups opposes plays, be careful. Frequently plays include situations which place some groups in a bad light or achieve humor through putting a member of a minority group in a ridiculous situation. Be sure your play

II. Use the Existing Pattern of Contact Between Groups

1. Find the go-betweens. Regardless of the depth of the chasm that separates groups there are always

doesn't ridicule one of the groups in your community. lines of communication, or bridges, connecting them. The go-betweens are persons who are recognized by the community as contacts and have prestige in both groups. This may be an organization such as the *Lulacs* (League of United Latin American Citizens) in the Southwest who represent Spanish-American people in state and community affairs and the officers of which are also recognized as leaders in the larger community on a par with the Anglo-Americans, or the go-between may be an individual of high standing in all groups. In one community with a large Polish population an attorney of Polish descent is recognized by the Poles as one who can be depended upon to look after their interests in the larger community. The other groups likewise look to him as the person who will explain things to the Polish settlement.

2. Discuss the proposal with the go-betweens. Explain your program to these go-betweens and seek their advice both as to how to reach the group they represent and how to get a community-wide action.

3. Find out the internal organization of the group. Frequently the internal solidarity and organization of minority groups is strong. If the organizer takes advantage of this existing strong organization, his work may be greatly facilitated.

4. Incorporate the suggestions of the go-betweens into the pattern of organization for your program. These are the people upon whom you must depend to smooth the way for you.

(a) In fitting the several groups into the larger community organization there are at least three possible patterns which may be followed.

(1) The community worker may use some existing intergroup organization.

(2) A new organization may be proposed which has representatives of all groups on a community committee. In this instance the go-betweens can be of great help in avoiding situations which might alienate the support of their groups.

(3) The worker may co-ordinate on an informal basis the efforts of the different groups.

(b) Reaching the people of the various groups.

(1) For each group use the leader-follower relations of that group. If the worker does not make use of existing organization, he is likely to fail in his efforts to reach the members of the divergent groups. Then the strong organization of the group may be used against him. A person who is approached by a leader whom he is accustomed to follow will respond more favorably than if approached by someone from outside his culture group. Wherever there are two culture groups there is likely to be a strong feeling of confidence within each group and suspicion if not fear of those outside. Moreover, such short-circuiting of the group leader may be interpreted as a threat to his prestige and result in opposition by his organization.

(2) Where local foreign-language newspapers or radio broadcasts provide a useful medium, see that they carry a carefully prepared announcement. The success of your program will be proportionate to the extent of the participation of members of all the groups all the way down the line.

*How to Mobilize
Urban Community Resources*

THE URBAN COMMUNITY is made up of a number of diverse social groups. In fact, the primary characteristic of the city is its tremendous social diversity of racial, nationality, class, age, interest, and other groups. Anyone who engages in a program of community development or improvement who does not keep this central fact of diversity in mind succeeds only by accident.

In fact, it may be a mistake to consider the large city as a community at all. As the city grows it adds a number of loosely integrated neighborhoods, subcommunities, or areas. It is more realistic, then, to think of the larger city as an *area* containing a number of more or less interdependent units, neighborhoods, and communities which are internally quite similar. The things that bind these groups together are the need for common public services, common economic facilities, and division of labor.

The larger the city grows, the greater is the need for its subareas to co-operate in attaining common services and goals. Since size itself makes personal and spontaneous co-operation on a continuous basis almost impossible, special associations are created to meet special needs. Thus, in a real sense, organizations and institutions, not personalities, run the life of the city. The spontaneous co-operation and flexibility possible among organizations of smaller localities where officers know

Guidepost 9 by William H. Form, Professor of Sociology, Michigan State College.

each other are almost impossible in the metropolis. Every need, if it is ever satisfied, is usually met with a new association. Since old organizations rarely expand to absorb new functions, the city suffers from organizational problems.

Consequently, the city may be envisioned as a complex of many special and general interest associations and institutions. Unlike smaller communities, which often suffer from underorganization, many cities suffer from overorganization, uneven organizational development, or poor integration of organizations. The first job of urban action-minded people, then, is to decide: (1) whether their problems are city-wide or local in character; (2) what organizations already exist on a city-wide or local basis.

Many well-meaning urban groups who think they see unmet social needs want to do something about them immediately. The best advice is to proceed with caution, for the urban death rate of new organizations is extremely high. Little is achieved if another association is added to the thousands that already exist.

I. Before You Start

Before an organization is launched at least six other paths to action should be tried.

1. Make a survey to be sure that the need you see is really not being met adequately by an existing organization. Almost surely some group interested in your problems will be found.

2. Exert pressure on such organizations to live up to their purposes. Much social action in cities is realized by pressure groups who are not afraid to recognize and use social power. Often merely bringing attention to

the existence of problems is sufficient to get action. The techniques of exerting pressure vary from publicity campaigns to threats of setting up competitive organizations.

3. Join or work through a sympathetic organization. It is often desirable for a citizen group to become a segment of an organization and attempt to widen or channel its energies. For example, the PTA, church groups, veterans organizations, and city centrals of labor unions are interested in community welfare. Not infrequently, all these associations need is information and invigorated leadership to launch programs of civic or local improvement.

4. Try to co-ordinate related organizations first. Often a task cannot be initiated and achieved because resources and personnel are inadequate. These are sometimes made available by trying to co-ordinate the activities of two or more interested parties. A citizen group can justify its existence by merely informing associations of the existence of related groups and providing initial contacts and liaisons.

5. Unsell opposing groups if possible. Many citizens blind themselves to the fact that some groups are actively blocking much needed social change. Before progress toward a goal can be made, opposition must be overcome. There is no alternative in such cases but to become a pressure group and join the struggle for power and influence.

6. As the last alternative, launch your special organization. Before this is done, however, an inventory of available money and willing personnel must be made. Failure to be successful may discourage many subsequent efforts.

II. Smaller Urban Areas

City-wide programs of improvement must be, almost of necessity, the task of co-operating private agencies or of the municipal government. Co-ordination is the key to the success of the first, and pressure to the success of the second. Although both techniques may be used in developing smaller areas, the individual private association can also be useful in this regard. No guidepost can be suggested which will be equally useful in organizational work in all sections of the city, because the city is composed of different kinds of social and cultural groups. To simplify the task of specifying techniques for community development, the city may be divided into the following sections:

1. The central business sections and the outlying or neighborhood business areas.

2. Areas of widest social diversity that surround the business districts.

3. Racial and nationality neighborhoods, made up of first and second-generation immigrants or rural migrants. These are mostly manual workers.

4. Older native middle-class areas, containing skilled, white-collar, executive, and professional workers.

5. Suburban and fringe areas of the city, where white-collar or mixed occupational groups live.

These areas vary in the amount of formal organizational life, the need for general improvement, and the techniques that can be used for successful local action.

1. The problems of the business district concern general appearance, physical deterioration, traffic flow, noise, and dirt. If citizen groups seek to improve the area, they must solicit and get the co-operation of local businessmen. Since the latter do not live in this area,

local pride is at a low ebb. In addition, improvements in the district involve rather large expenditures of money. Apathy and expense make it advisable for interested parties to work with the municipal government and its planning agencies in the redevelopment of the area.

2. Attacking problems of the belts around the business districts presents even greater difficulties. Three main reasons are responsible for this situation. First, this area has the greatest amount of physical and social deterioration. Second, the population there is the most diversified in the city. Third, social and organizational life is at the lowest ebb. Housing, health, crime, vice, recreational, and economic problems are most acute in this area. The physical and social resources of its residents are so meager that outside assistance and counsel are necessary. No one should attempt working in this area without first becoming acquainted with the pioneer efforts of the Chicago Area Project.

The main problems are finding the small culturally homogeneous areas in the district, learning the point of view of the residents, providing the important minimum facilities for youth and adult groups, gaining the confidence of local informal leaders no matter who they may be, and getting these leaders to recognize the problems of the area, and to use their efforts and influence in meeting the needs of community development. Only small achievable problems should be attacked until the feeling of hope and success is built up. In the meantime the help of the municipal government must be sought to engage in the physical reconstruction of the area.

3. The problems in the areas where racial and na-

tionality groups predominate are enormous but easier to solve. The needs of these areas are similar to those in the belt surrounding the business district. The techniques which work there may be applied with greater success in the ethnic areas, because of the existence of much informal and some formal organization. It is wise to get the backing of these groups in any program, for they have the real power in the area. A genuine appreciation of their culture, values, and goals is necessary to action. Endorsement or participation of two groups is usually requisite for successful community action. They are the race or nationality societies and the labor union or informal occupational groups. Both the union and the ethnic societies are accepted locally. Their officers have local prestige, organizational skill, and knowledge of the informal network of social relations in the area.

Not infrequently these groups oppose the power of local factory managers and the school officials, for they are outsiders. If the co-operation of the factory managers, union, ethnic societies, and the school is impossible to obtain, it is usually wiser to work with the union and the ethnic societies. It is more important to get these groups and the local church groups, athletic clubs, ward political machines, and youth groups to recognize their community of interests than to succeed in establishing a new agency or program. Co-operation in rebuilding community life will go farther when the local people and their institutions recognize their common needs and goals.

4. The older native middle-class areas of the city are highly organized in both the formal and informal sense. Their citizens have the highest degree of com-

munity awareness and local pride. Unlike other groups in the city, they tend to create formal associations on the least pretext. The problem of the community-minded individual is to resist the reflex of starting a new association. His jobs should be: (a) make a sober analysis of the local resources, (b) discourage wasteful duplication of effort, and (c) foster the co-ordination of organizations in line with a well-thought-out *plan*. Only in this way may the natural integration of the area be improved.

5. The problems of the suburban communities are similar to those of the well-settled native areas of the city. One of the main differences between the two is that the suburbanite must participate in the social life of two communities: the business life of the city and the social life of the suburb. Since this is a difficult task for men, the suburban community life tends to be dominated by women who have the organizational reflex mentioned above. The problem is to break this female monopoly by encouraging men to take time from business affairs to join local groups in their community tasks.

The urban fringe is composed of suburbanites of all classes, farmers, and tradesmen. Fringe areas are in process of becoming neighborhoods. They are the least formally or informally organized sections of the metropolitan community. Consequently the task that confronts those who seek to improve life in the fringe is the same that faces pioneers everywhere, namely, the *development* of organizational life. The needs of the area are many, including public utilities, roads, zoning, recreational, and other facilities. Unlike other areas, the sooner *any* organization succeeds in bringing people into face-to-face contacts, the better. Since the social composition of the fringe is so varied, however, organizational efforts must be designed to meet the social needs of all to be successful. Other material needs may be satisfied after the social ones are met.

In conclusion, the large urban community is made up of a number of subareas that differ widely on many scores. Successful community action can be attained only when participants realize the common as well as the distinguishing attributes of city dwellers. This brief guidepost should be supplemented by additional reading before organizational attempts become mature. The following represent minimal sources which should be consulted and supplemented:

American Journal of Soliology, May, 1941. Articles by W. L. Warner, S. D. Alinsky, and others are valuable.

S. T. Kimball, *The New Social Frontier, the Fringe,* Special Bulletin 360, Michigan State College Experiment Station, June, 1949.

Merton, West, Jahoda, Selvin, *Social Policy and Social Research in Housing,* Association Press, 1951.

L. Wirth, *Community Planning for Peacetime Living,* Stanford University Press, 1946.

You and Your Neighborhood, a Primer, Revere Copper and Brass, Inc., New York, 1944.

GUIDEPOST
10

How the Church Can Contribute to Community Programs

THE CHURCH can be one of the most effective forces for stimulating wholesome community

Guidepost 10 by Mark Rich, Professor of Rural Church, Bible College of Missouri.

life. In history and currently, the most influential churches are community-minded churches and are closely identified with the total interests of community life. The church exists for the community and has an important role in working with constructive forces for building a good community.

I. What Does the Church Have to Contribute?

1. *The pastor, a leader.* The pastor can be a leader in community affairs. A well-trained minister has many skills and techniques which equip him for such leadership. A poorly trained man can improve himself by attending conferences, by making proper contacts, and by reading. The work of the church and the community are so closely related that every pastor has some time for this leadership.

2. *Church leaders should be community leaders.* The church can direct its members to devote themselves to wholesome community activity and service. The worship, teaching, and idealism of the church can inspire a wholesome interest in community progress.

3. *Makes equipment available.* The church can make equipment available for community use. The church may be well furnished with dining room, social hall, meeting and recreation rooms, and other equipment. These should be available to the community, usually without cost.

4. *Church, an energizing force.* The church can build morale for community living. It is an energizing force, giving people a deep faith in the possibilities of a better community. Young people in particular can be led to see the advantages of improving their home community.

5. *Helps people put first things first in program planning.* The church can help the community planners appreciate constructive programs. This appraisal of programs will determine the nature of the activities in which people engage. A community in which people put first things first is likely to see that professional recreational leadership is more important than a large community hall without provision for leadership. Such a community will vote for a music teacher in the high school before spending $2,500 on Fourth of July fireworks. It will employ a swimming instructor rather than license a roadhouse. It will think a library more important than a statue or a cannon on the square.

6. *Emphasizes enduring values.* The church will keep before the community the long-time truths and the enduring values, such as character, integrity, and good will. It will help the people keep in mind the valuable lessons from the past and give them a sense of responsibility for the future.

II. How Can a Church Most Effectively Make These Contributions?

1. *Be aware of the community.* In order to serve the community, the church must recognize that the community exists. This community has geographic boundaries, and the people within these boundaries are associated in economic relationships, in culture, and sociability. The interest of all should be the interest of each. By giving spiritual meaning to these relationships the church will believe in the community as much as it believes in itself.

2. *Have a program of community service.* The church should have a program of service for the com-

munity. Its regular services meet part of the community needs. But there are other necessary forms of service. A church at Titonka, Iowa, which led the community toward the solution of the tenantry problem did a notable service. Another church served well when it organized a vacation school in the poor neighborhood on the fringe of the community. Another helped finance a recreation program on the local playground. Churches such as these encourage their members to take part in wholesome community activities.

3. *Foster co-operative relationships among churches.* The church can serve by working with other churches in the community. The good will that grows out of these relationships will in itself give strong unity to the community. The ministers may have regular planning meetings. There may also be a council of representatives from the churches which promotes united church programs on a community basis.

4. *Co-operate with local organizations in community affairs.* The church can have active representation on the community council. If there is no council, there can be informal planning with community agencies. A "future dates" column may be listed in the weekly newspaper. The church leaders will graciously help adjust conflicts in schedules. The church will recognize that its divine origin gives it no priority in standing, but commissions it a serving group along with other agencies.

5. *Promote comradeship.* The church can minimize cleavages by promoting comradeship and "togetherness" in community life.

6. *Be true to its mission.* The church can also serve the community in a unique way by being true to its

own purposes. That church which in public gatherings, in daily lives of its members, and in its constant good works, remains true to its mission will do much in giving to a community those ideals and practices by which it will grow strong.

GUIDEPOST
11

How the Public School Can Serve the Community

THE PIONEER COMMUNITY planned, built, operated, and controlled its own school. It was truly a folk school of, by, and for the local people. As the school has come of age, the part played by local citizens has been gradually reduced. The work of the school has become more complex. The building is erected by a contractor, the teacher is technically trained, the curriculum is largely fashioned by forces outside the community, state regulations have increased, and often community boundaries have changed without a corresponding adjustment in school districts. These changes have tended to separate the school from the community. To counteract this trend there has been a definite movement in recent years to develop a school which grows out of and serves the life of the community.

I. The Responsibility of the School

1. *To the educational needs of the pupils it enrolls.* The school's major responsibility is to give the pupils the training they need to be good citizens. The value

Guidepost 11 by Frank W. Cyr, Teachers College, Columbia University.

of any activity or program in which the school engages must be measured in terms of this purpose.

2. *To the youths and adults.* Probably the finest education is that in which both children and adults learn and work together on a common program. The provision for special educational services to adults is increasing.

3. *To other agencies of the community.* The school must work with other agencies of the community on educational problems of mutual concern and in many cases take the leadership in co-operative programs. It has a responsibility for helping to develop and carry on the kinds of community organizations and community programs which will make the community a better place in which to live. It is particularly effective when universal participation is needed since it works in all communities and has wide contacts within each.

II. How Can the School Discharge Its Responsibility?

1. *Through the pupils.* The most important avenue of participation is through the youth and adults regularly enrolled. They are in daily contact with their families and other groups in their out-of-school activities. The work of the children therefore can be readily geared into programs for community development or programs of national significance. Community life should have an integral place in the work of the school.

2. *Through the staff.*

(a) The staff can strengthen community life through its regular educational work within the school.

(b) It can aid by taking part in community activities and by exploring possible ways in which such activities can produce real educational value.

(c) The best use is made of the professional staff when it has a definite part in the *initial planning* of policies and programs.

(d) The principal or superintendent occupies a strategic place in the community and should be asked to advise in all major community undertakings.

(e) The nonprofessional members of the school staff—janitors, bus drivers, and mechanics—are often in position to make an important contribution to community understanding of the school.

3. *Through the school plant.* The school building and grounds provide an important resource for housing community activities. It represents a large capital investment on which maximum returns should be secured through wide use. Possibilities are the use of the auditorium for community meetings, the gymnasium for physical activities, the home economics room for home demonstration projects, the shop for building and repair, the smaller rooms for committee and group meetings, the kitchen and lunch room for luncheons, suppers, and banquets, and the school grounds for picnics and summer playgrounds. In addition the school increasingly is used to house the public library, health clinics, recreational programs, and similar activities.

III. Selecting Activities in Which the School Should Participate

1. The school should be careful to use energies and resources where they will count the most. It must be

flexible and responsible to new needs but it cannot rush in all directions at once.

2. *The school is an educational and not an action agency.* It must be concerned that any program in which it participates provides effective learning and does not exploit the children for some immediate objective such as producing food, raising funds, or collecting information. It must recognize that such action programs may be significant educational experiences and insure that the maximum educational values are realized.

3. *The school should aid in programs of value to the community.* Such programs must be of sufficient constructive value to justify the attention of the school.

4. *The pupils must participate in planning programs.* If a program is to yield greatest returns, the pupils who participate must have some part in planning it, realize its importance, and have some chance of carrying it through successfully. They will definitely grow themselves as a result of such an experience.

IV. Barriers to School Participation

Every agency in the community has certain limitations to the part it can best play. The school cannot move more rapidly than the majority of the community members are willing, and it is limited by what the staff have the time and energy to do. The school is sometimes limited by a board which does not truly represent a cross section of community life and may tend to discourage the type of education most suited to majority needs.

Probably the greatest limitation on the school's usefulness at the present time is the fact that, in many areas, communities have changed and community boundaries expanded but schools and school districts have remained the same. *The most effective school is the one which has been set up to serve the natural sociological community in which it is located.*

GUIDEPOST

12

How to Organize
a Community Chest

A COMMUNITY CHEST is a co-operative organization of citizens and welfare agencies. It has two chief functions: (1) It raises funds for the affiliated agencies, through a community-wide appeal, and distributes them according to a systematic budget procedure. (2) It promotes co-operative planning, co-ordination, and administration of the community's social welfare, health, and recreation services. The direct responsibility for this function may be carried by a Community Welfare Council (also called Council of Social Agencies or Council for Social Planning).

A Community Welfare Council is a voluntary association of citizens who represent both the tax-supported and the voluntary social welfare, health, and recreational agencies, or who serve as interested individuals. It carries primary responsibility for the planning and co-ordination of the entire community social welfare program.

What community interests should participate in the

Guidepost 12 adapted with permission from *Organizing and Operating a Community Chest,* Bulletin No. 143, 1949, Community Chests and Councils of America, Inc.

Chest? The more the better! In most cities the Chest is an organization through which all religious, racial, economic and professional interests in the community unite in unselfish service for the common good. Such unity can come only when all these interests have full confidence in the objectives and administration of the Chest. Ordinarily they will not have this kind of confidence unless they share responsibility for the management of the Chest.

I. Important Preliminaries to Organization

1. *Be sure that representative leaders share in the first plans of formation.* The question of organizing a Chest usually receives its first formal consideration from a small but representative and influential group of leaders. The points of view of both small and large contributors as well as of prospective participating agencies should be represented. The group should not be large, but no one with a genuine interest in the project should be excluded. Representatives of labor should be among them, in order that the important large group of working people share in the first plans of formation.

2. *Conduct basic studies.* Before a Chest can be successfully launched it is important to make some basic studies of the needs, services, and resources of the community. Points to be covered should be

(a) the area to be served and solicited together with facts about its population, economic resources, etc.

(b) the organizations which are potential members of the Chest and a description of their services. (Do these services extend over the entire area to be served?)

(c) the variety and scope of existing health and welfare programs, including those carried on by the tax-supported agencies, county, state or federal.

(d) the total income and expenditures of the existing agencies for the past year; the extent to which the organizations have capital resources or debts, debts for current expenditures, or surpluses.

(e) a list of the voluntary contributors to each of the organizations for the past year to be put on master cards, one for each person.

3. *When to go ahead.* Experience has shown that the decision to organize a Chest may well be justified:

(a) If the social agencies which would logically qualify for participation in the Chest are favorably disposed toward its initiation.

(b) If major contributors or groups of contributors and top lay leaders approve the idea.

(c) If the service program of the prospective Chest agencies extends over the entire territory proposed for solicitation, or there is reasonable promise that it may do so.

(d) If the total amount to be raised warrants providing professional administrative direction—the salary of a full-time executive preferably, or at least the part-time employment of a consultant.

4. *Keep the discussion going.* During the process of the initial study it is recommended that meetings be held at appropriate times when representatives of the social agencies and other leaders in the community will discuss together the facts discovered.

The importance of organized labor participation in the Chest and Council warrants sincere efforts to draw adequate representation from those groups into preliminary discussions. The hours at which meetings are held are a controlling factor to working people.

5. *Allow sufficient time for organization.* It is further recommended that in case it is decided to organize a Chest, the organization be completed at least three months before the financial campaign is launched.

II. Principles of Organization

1. *Work out a careful plan for setting up the Chest.* Three suggested steps are the following:

(a) *The Community Committee.* If informal discussion indicates that it is advisable to proceed, an acceptable method is to invite a committee of fifty to one hundred persons to a meeting to discuss the questions of organizing a Chest. The individuals composing the smaller group that first discussed the idea can prepare the invitation list to make sure it includes all important agency, economic, geographic, cultural, religious, press, and other groups. They may also prepare a statement setting forth the pros and cons of organization, to be presented at the larger meeting or mailed out in advance in order to give those present a basis for intelligent and directed discussion of the idea.

(b) *The First General Meeting.* It may be called by the mayor, the chairman of the Welfare Council, president of the Chamber of Commerce or by any other person, group, or organization that will earmark the meeting as a community event in which no particular individual or group is trying to railroad an idea. Sufficient time should be allowed for free discussion from the floor and for answering questions. Communities may find it helpful to invite the president and executive of a nearby Chest to be present to answer questions.

As the meeting proceeds, the chairman will be able

to gauge whether general sentiment is for or against organizing a Chest, and can decide whether to call for a motion in favor of proceeding with plans. Organization plans can usually be speeded if additional motions are passed electing temporary officers such as a chairman and secretary, and appointing a small organizing committee to draft the legal documents, prepare a slate of nominees for the first board, and attend to other details, with instructions to report at a second meeting of the large committee.

In order to make certain that the organizing committee is sufficiently representative of community interests and includes persons who have the skills necessary for the preparation of the legal documents, it is usually wise to have in mind before the first large meeting names of persons who will be asked to serve. When prepared, the proposed articles of incorporation and constitution can be mailed to all members of the large committee well ahead of the second meeting. This will give the members an opportunity to study the material, and the boards of the agencies who are going to participate sufficient time to take formal action.

(c) *Formal Organization.* Adoption of a constitution and election of the first board of directors can then take place at the second general meeting. It becomes the responsibility of the board to elect permanent officers, appoint necessary committees and formally incorporate the organization.

2. *Secure adequate finances for first campaign.* The minor expenses of preliminary organization probably will not be a problem. When formal organization has been completed and plans for administration and the

coming campaign must proceed, however, adequate finances to carry the organization through the first campaign must be secured.

There are several possible methods of securing these funds. One method is to have several of the individuals and business corporations who are potential big givers either make their campaign contributions at once or agree to serve as underwriters for a bank loan. This accomplished, the organization can proceed to make necessary arrangements for executive leadership, offices, supplies, and clerical assistance which cannot be secured on any other basis.

3. *Keep in touch with those experienced in formation and operation of Community Chests.*

(a) Talk with leaders from other cities where Chests have proven successful.

(b) Talk with local social, health, and recreation workers whose professional experience elsewhere has acquainted them with the purposes and techniques connected with Community Chests.

(c) Secure expert assistance from *Community Chests and Councils of America, Inc.,* 155 East 44 Street, New York 17. They can supply much-needed information upon such points as details of articles of incorporation and constitution, making out Chest budgets and allocation of funds, conducting campaigns, handling publicity, administration of the Chest through the governing board, qualifications needed for the executive, agency relationships, etc.

How to Organize
a Community Council

A COMMUNITY COUNCIL is one type of organization for voluntary effort to solve problems of common concern in a community. Break this definition down and we have the following basic ideas:

It is *voluntary.* Participation is not compulsory. The council's actions do not have the force of law, but only the power of public opinion.

Common concern means concern with those problems of community life beyond the ability of the individual citizen, family, or single organization to solve alone.

And what is a community? For our purposes here, a community is an area—any area—in which people are willing and ready to work together on a co-operative basis, to get what they want. This may be a neighborhood, a town and country community, a school district, a village or city, a county, or any combination of these.

I. Who Belongs To a Community Council?

The membership of a community council usually includes (1) delegates or representatives of civic, professional, educational, religious, agricultural, labor, and business organizations; (2) delegates or representatives of public and voluntary community service agencies; and (3) individual members chosen for their interest, knowledge, or competence in civic affairs and not representing any particular organization.

Guidepost 13 adapted from *Teamwork in the Community,* Wisconsin Community Organization Committee, Madison, July, 1951, pages 4-10. Used by permission.

All economic and social groups, as well as geographic areas, should be urged to participate. A community council cannot get results if it leaves out groups which have a genuine interest in community improvement

and direct lines of communication to citizens. The main idea, when it comes to membership, is to *get* participation, not to *limit* it.

The following is a suggested list of agencies and organizations for a community council:

Agricultural organizations
Business and professional organizations
Educational institutions and services
Fraternal and service clubs

Governmental agencies and departments
Health and welfare agencies
Human relations groups
Industry
Labor organizations
Patriotic organizations
Racial and nationality groups
Religious organizations
Women's groups
Youth organizations

A community council needs youth for its own sake and for the sake of youth. In return for receiving new ideas and fresh enthusiasm it will give youth a training ground for future responsible leadership.

While it is important to include professional staff of member agencies, the success of a community council in winning community support will depend most upon strong citizenship participation.

II. What Does a Community Council Do?

No two community councils will be exactly alike in program, but they share the general purpose of improving all phases of community life. The most vital part of a community council's job is to study problems and needs and to plan co-operatively to meet them. It does this by:

1. Encouraging informed citizen participation
2. Fact-finding
3. Developing public understanding and support
4. Co-ordinating community activities and services
5. Co-operative action

Encouraging Informed Citizen Participation. Citizen

participation in community life is the foundation of a strong democracy. But an active citizen must be a well-informed citizen. A truly representative community council educates for civic leadership; for example,

1. Through a fact-finding committee to study needs and resources of a community.

2. Through a radio panel about recreational services.

3. Through directing a poll of youth and adult employment opportunities.

Fact-Finding. One of the most valuable things a community council can do is continually and carefully to gather facts about its community—its health, human relations, education, recreation, religious, economic, and welfare needs—and to agree on how these needs can best be met. If a council does nothing more than to study such facts and present them fairly and completely, it has proved its worth.

A council will find it advantageous to call in consultants from outside the community to direct or assist in making fact-finding studies; for example,

1. A study to find out how widely boys and girls are participating in the program of youth agencies. Such a study might result in the discovery that certain age or racial groups are not being served, or that some areas have more than enough youth agencies, while others have too few.

2. A study of the public health nursing activities carried on by a private agency, the health department and the schools. This might reveal a duplication of services for control of communicable disease and a neglect of bedside care. In this case, the community might agree to establish one central nursing service or otherwise plan for total service coverage.

3. A study of the zoning problems in relation to adequate housing.   This might result in improved living conditions for families.

Developing Public Understanding and Support. A community council stimulates public awareness of community problems, develops an understanding of how the community deals with these problems, and gains support for the necessary services and programs. How? By sponsoring public meetings and forums; maintaining speakers' bureaus; distributing studies and reports; and getting publicity through the press and radio. Community understanding of needs and services develops through council delegates' reports to their own organizations.   Activities a council might undertake include:

1. Publishing a directory of the community's health, welfare, education and recreation resources.

2. Issuing a report on health and other community needs.

3. Sponsoring a family life institute or conferences of community improvement.

4. Arranging for newspaper articles or radio programs of an informational or educational nature.

5. Providing up-to-date information on business, industry, and employment opportunities.

Co-ordinating Community Activities and Services. Community councils provide a meeting ground for people from different public or voluntary agencies or organizations to come together, share their experiences, understand each other's viewpoints, and agree on some definite plans. By working voluntarily on joint projects, community leaders learn to lift their eyes from their own specialized interests and take a look at the whole community.   When advisable, they assign parts of the total job to suitable organizations so that people will receive the best possible services with the least duplication of effort, time, and money.

A community council also co-ordinates by bringing old and new services into proper balance. By its understanding of all the facts it is more likely to reflect the best judgment of all concerned.

Councils often provide some common service to member organizations unable to achieve it alone. Examples of co-ordinating activities are:

1. Arranging meetings at which each organization can describe its purpose and program to other organizations.

2. Creating a Christmas Bureau to co-ordinate the flood of spontaneous giving.

3. Getting out a calendar of future events and meetings to help individual organizations avoid conflicts in dates.

4. Developing a co-operative training program for volunteer leaders of all leisure-time organizations.

Co-operative Action. After considering the facts and agreeing upon a logical course of action, the council takes steps to carry out its plans. This may require modifying an existing service or developing an entirely new one. In any case, interested citizens and organizations arrive at a joint decision.

Council action may mean conference and negotiation with officials administering the services. It may mean consultation with the group which appropriates funds such as Community Chest, or county, village, or town boards, or the city council.

Councils should not generally operate community services directly, though they may do so occasionally on a temporary demonstration basis. Co-operative activities include:

1. Negotiating with two existing agencies or organizations for a merger of their services or projects.

2. Holding conferences with school authorities to work out plans for use of school buildings for summer recreation.

3. Presenting to the city council recommendations for improvement of a swimming beach or pool.

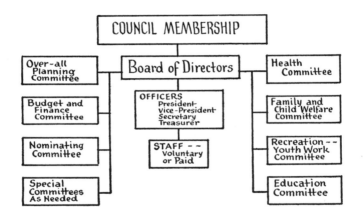

III. What Kind of Organization Structure Is Necessary?

The council should develop its own pattern of organization and not attempt to adopt that of another community. The success of a council does not depend upon a fixed pattern but rather upon its ability to deal with its own community needs. It is well to keep the organization simple and flexible, with an executive committee or board, necessary officers, and committees as needed to carry out specific tasks or projects. Particularly in a small council it is unwise to develop too many standing committees.

While it is important that a council adopt a constitution and by-laws, overemphasis upon this in the developmental stage, to the neglect of a program based upon community needs, may result in loss of interest on the part of the membership.

Leadership. The success of a council depends on several things, but perhaps most important of all is the quality of its leadership. The council able to arrange for some paid staff service, even if only part-time, is fortunate. For such staff help, the council might look to one of the following sources:

1. A public or private agency that will permit one of its employees to function as council secretary.

2. Staff of a Community Chest.

3. A retired person with interest and special ability.

Selection or election of officers, directors, and committee chairmen must be more than a haphazard process. A nominating committee is one way of getting good results. Council leadership should meet the following qualifications:

1. Have sincere faith in people.

2. Have broad vision and a community point of view.

3. Have ability to get people to work together in a democratic way.

4. Command wide respect in the community.

5. Give enough time to do the job required.

*How to Develop
a Community Recreation Program*

RECREATION PROGRAMS cannot be planned according to a standard pattern; they must be related to the special needs and interests of the people. In some communities local groups can best promote recreation by initiating and conducting specific activities; in others by co-operating with existing recreation agencies in making their programs more effective. Establishment of a municipal recreation department may be the most worthwhile objective for a local organization.

I. Preliminary Steps in Starting a Recreation Program

1. First, consider whether your group should tackle the problem singlehanded or whether it should enlist the co-operation of other local agencies. One organization may successfully undertake a limited project such as a boy's softball league or a day camp program, but a more representative group can best launch a community-wide program.

2. If your organization decides that others should share in the project, it should approach these local groups and request them to appoint representatives to a recreation committee to study the problem and develop a plan of action.

3. In any case an inventory of local resources is advisable. This involves finding out what recreation

Guidepost 14 adapted with permission from *Recreation for Your Community*, published by the National Recreation Association.

facilities and programs are already available. Make a list of the properties owned by city and school authorities, churches, industries, and private and commercial organizations, that are being used for recreation or that are suitable for such use. Record the various recreation facilities at each of these properties. Compile, too, a list of the local authorities, clubs, and organizations that offer leisure-time programs and record the nature and extent of the activities comprising them.

4. Make a survey of local recreation interests and desires. This may be an informal inquiry among selected groups, or questionnaires may be circulated among school children and adults, designed to reveal the types of activities desired by the local residents.

5. Study the local and state legislation relating to recreation in order to learn what powers the local authorities have to establish and finance a public recreation program.

6. Analyze social conditions such as substandard housing, juvenile delinquency cases, street accidents, and infant mortality. The findings will reveal the sections of the community where the need for recreation is most urgent.

II. The Establishment of a Municipal Recreation Program

1. After the preliminary steps have been taken, work out a program with the help of local townspeople and recreation specialists. Consult, for instance, the field staff of the National Recreation Association, 315 Fourth Avenue, New York 10, or recreation specialists at state universities and other educational institutions.

2. The public must be informed about the proposal,

and public interest and support must be secured. Several methods of accomplishing this are suggested.

3. Arrange one or more public meetings and publicize them widely. Send notices to all local organizations and ask them to appoint representatives to attend. Invite the city and school authorities to be present. At the meetings summarize the committee's findings, interpret the needs that have been disclosed, and present the proposed plan of action. Make it clear that suggestions about modifications will be welcome, in order that the final plan may represent truly the will of the people and merit their support. If possible, arrange to have an experienced recreation worker present to answer technical questions and to report what other communities are doing. Two or more meetings may be needed before a satisfactory plan and program can be worked out.

4. Request the appropriate local authority, which may be the city council, selectmen, park board, or school board, to take the necessary action to get the program started. If the plan includes the appointment of a recreation commission, as is frequently the case, the local governing authority must:

(a) Pass an ordinance or resolution creating a recreation commission and setting forth its powers and duties. In most states this action is authorized specifically under state enabling legislation.

(b) Appropriate funds for the work of the commission.

(c) Provide an office for the superintendent of recreation or other personnel when employed by the commission.

(d) Turn over to the commission the control and

use of city-owned areas designed or suitable for recreation.

5. Widespread publicity relating to the recreation plan is essential. Articles in newspapers, interviews with leading citizens, radio broadcasts, brief addresses at meetings of organizations, children's parades, posters, showings of recreation films are all useful. The nature and scope of the publicity program will depend upon the local situation and the attitude of the local authorities. Resolutions passed by organizations urging action by the authorities may be helpful.

6. Since funds may not be available for recreation in the current city, park, or school budget, it may be necessary to raise funds privately for the work of the commission until the end of the fiscal year.

7. After a recreation program has been established under public auspices, there is still work to be done by a citizens' committee or advisory recreation council. Such a group can continue to study the community's recreation needs, help with recreation projects, interpret recreation, and support the commission in its work.

III. How to Help a Recreation Department

1. Local organizations can appoint members to a citizens' committee or council; they may even be represented on the official commission.

2. They can keep informed about the work of the department, offer suggestions for its program, and support its budget requests.

3. Appropriations are never sufficient to do all that the department is called upon to perform, so that organizations can furnish funds for special events or purposes. They may, for example, buy the awards

for the coaster derby; furnish transportation for an outing for playground children; purchase seeds for a home garden program; or arrange a dinner when the annual sports awards are presented.

4. In case of a campaign for a bond issue for a new swimming pool, athletic field, or playground, local organizations can pass resolutions, circulate petitions, or otherwise help in securing favorable action. Local referendum campaigns for a special recreation mill tax can be supported in a like manner.

5. Opportunities for the use of volunteers are open in every community. Organizations can enlist members to render volunteer services as athletic coaches, as storytellers, as instructors in crafts, music, or sports, as hobby club leaders, and as officials at games, tournaments, and special events.

6. Organizations can interest themselves in helping the community secure more adequate recreation facilities. When a new school is proposed, they can urge the acquisition of a site that is large enough to serve as a neighborhood playground and the provision of indoor facilities that are designed for both school and community use. They can also work for the provision of recreation areas and facilities in real estate subdivisions and large-scale housing developments.

GUIDEPOST

15   *How to Plan for Industrial Development*

A COMMUNITY THAT just "grows like Topsy" may easily grow worse. Every growing com-

Guidepost 15 adapted from *A Guide to Community Industrial Development in New England,* prepared by the Industrial Development Committee of the New England Council, Boston.

munity should have a well-balanced plan for its future. Such a plan is the responsibility of a planning commission. At the same time, a separate committee may assist greatly in fostering industrial development in proper relation to the general program. By alert and aggressive action such a committee may lead in the acquisition of new industry, thereby providing opportunities to keep young people at home.

I. Basic Ingredients

1. There must be one or two individuals in the community who see the need for concerted action and will provide the original impetus to organize . . .

2. A well-integrated, widely representative committee which will provide leadership for . . .

3. Widespread community support and participation in a development program which will require . . .

4. Diligent, persistent, volunteer effort and . . .

5. Patience.

Caution, too, is a necessary ingredient.

1. "Politics" have spelled failure in many past cases. If the community industrial development effort becomes identified with a single political character or party, its future becomes uncertain. The objectives are nonpartisan; community support should be.

2. Money strengthens but also corrupts. Financial support that is derived by widespread, voluntary contribution owes an obligation only to the general community. It will be cautiously spent. Tax-based funds habitually come and go easily.

3. Haste is a pitfall. Community industrial development is a long-range process that is most successful when carefully planned and executed.

II. The Committee For Industrial Development

Many communities have found a separate Industrial Development Committee a suitable method of organizing community effort. While a local chamber of commerce or other civic group may initially sponsor such a committee, its membership should promptly be broadened to include all important segments of the community.

1. *The Committee membership* should include three general types of people. Leading interested citizens should be involved so that public attention and interest will be assured. Representatives of labor (organized and unorganized), manufacturers, tradesmen, bankers, lawyers, ministers, educators, and public officials should be included as a method of securing their divergent viewpoints on common matters.

Representatives of civic associations should be included as a channel of communication with and support from their organizations. The size of the committee will vary with the size of the community.

2. *The Committee organization* should be flexible to meet the tasks that arise. Generally, it is advisable to have a chairman and fairly small executive committee composed of chairmen of subcommittees. Possible subcommittees are:

(a) *Finance:* To raise funds for the necessary operating expenses of the committee and possibly to secure contributions and develop a financial plan if a large effort is to be undertaken.

(b) *Survey:* To plan, organize, and conduct an industrial survey of the community and keep its information up to date.

(c) *Advertising and Education:* To publicize the work of the committee—both to make industrial contacts and keep the community informed.

(d) *Zoning:* To study and promote planned land use in conjunction with the community planning commission if any.

III. *The Industrial Survey*

At the initial meeting of a Community Industrial Development Committee, three interwoven questions will loom large.

What Do We Have?

What Do We Want?

How Do We Get It?

The answers to all three questions depend on the results of a survey.

1. A community survey, organized and conducted by the community residents, may be as broad or as limited as desired. For the purposes of industrial development the survey is designed to answer such questions as the following:

(a) What industry is operating in the community and what obstacles impede its expansion?

(b) What resources, such as land, buildings, labor, materials, markets, transportation, power, public facilities, etc., does this community have to offer a prospective firm?

(c) What activity should we undertake to improve the attractiveness of this community to new firms?

2. A survey to answer such questions is necessarily quite complicated since it involves the technical needs of manufacturers. However, the process is easily understandable and has been reduced to a checklist rou-

tine that insures adequate coverage and sensible tabulation of the results. The Industrial Development Committee of the New England Council will provide checklists and survey descriptions to interested communities, as will your own state planning board.

3. Once the survey is completed it must be analyzed to determine what particular local industries should be encouraged to grow and what type of new concerns are adapted to the community. Sometimes it will be found that a local firm could easily provide additional jobs with some assistance from the Committee. On occasion it will be found that the community is a "natural" location for a particular type industry. In any event, the effect on the community of a particularly desired firm should be carefully appraised in terms of the burdens imposed and benefits derived.

IV. Steps in Developing Industry

Communities have devised manifold ways to increase industrial jobs in light of findings of industrial surveys. Some of the successful devices are:

(1) Improvement of business climate in the community by supplying better schools, roads, water supply, industrial waste and sewerage disposal, more recreation facilities, understandable and reasonable tax, license and zoning laws, and economical, efficient local government.

(2) Developing a plan for securing new industry by contacting and negotiating with firms outside the community to encourage them to locate a plant in the community.

(3) Providing contacts between management and

local, regional, state, and federal industrial agencies whose specialists will help in locating prospective new firms.

(4) Planning and developing an industrial district zoned for manufacturers. Such provisions for roads, utilities, and fire protection impress new firms with the advantages of selecting a community that is actively preparing for expansion.

(5) Establishing an Industrial Foundation to help provide land and buildings for local firms to expand in and to house new firms seeking rented manufacturing space.

(6) Providing specialized consulting services for existing and new firms such as engineering studies, marketing studies, help in improving accounting systems, better record keeping, and advice on labor relations.

Industrial Development agencies that specialize in securing new concerns for communities are your best bet for locating prospects. The local electric or gas company, the local bank, the railroad, trucking, and airline companies servicing your region, state planning and development agencies, state chambers of commerce, U. S. Department of Commerce, regional banks, and (in New England) the Industrial Department of the New England Council can and will help.

Remember, the key to success is to have one qualified person with up-to-the-minute facts arranged for the one prospective customer and a follow-up method for every lead. If the new prospect desires to meet more members of the community, a selected group should be prepared to meet on short notice and ready to sell the community; but, only to a prospect who promises to become an asset and to share community responsibilities. To bring in a firm not adapted to the community is worse than failing to secure the new prospect.

How to Secure Wider
16 *Participation in Community Activities*

OUR SYSTEM OF representative government has allowed the individual to delegate many responsibilities to others. This has resulted, with most of us, in our leaving those obligations entirely in the hands of elected representatives, whose days are so short and whose numbers are so few that the immediate routine of duty shuts out the larger problems.

I. Community Leadership Is Borne by Too Few People

To supplement the services of government, most communities have organizations of one kind or another to care for the needy, encourage and guide the younger generation, debate questions of general interest, etc., etc. It is these organizations—community chests, child welfare agencies, civic clubs, boards of commerce, forums, and dozens of others—which largely determine the development or retardation of a community.

1. *More manpower needed.* The work they do is magnificent. But in the evolution of the community under representative government we have reached the point where their combined efforts are insufficient. The problems of today call for more manpower.

Guidepost 16 by J. A. Estes, Past President, Lexington, Kentucky, Rotary Club and Presidents' Round Table.

At the present stage of our development, about 10 per cent of the people perform about 90 per cent of the nonprofessional community work. The goal should be the enlistment of 100 per cent of the people in the general project of community improvement.

Manifestly this goal is unattainable. But, just as a drawing in proper perspective has a vanishing point which, though not actually shown, lends unity to the picture, so will a well-organized community keep in mind the interests of *all* its citizens and, as nearly as possible, draw from each of them some contribution of effort toward the general good. Though the goal is beyond reach, it provides a direction—and the more closely it is approached the greater the improvement possible.

2. *Prevention better than cure.* With only a small percentage of the population active in projects having to do with the general welfare, small specific improvements may be undertaken occasionally—a playground, a street widening, a new agency—but most of the effort will be expended in charity of one kind or another. Charity, of course, is essential. It helps to pick up the wreckage of broken lives. But it can do very little to change the situation which produced the breakage. In the long run, though the initial cost is higher in terms of planning, work, and money, it is cheaper and better to provide the conditions for security and happiness than to care for the victims of an environment which automatically produces many victims. Playgrounds and recreation centers, for instance, are more economical than jails; safety precautions are better than hospitals.

3. *All kinds of people are able to help.* In most communities the lead is taken by representatives of banks,

utility companies, factories, stores, prominent farmers, members of the professions, and their wives and daughters. These people work through community agencies, civic clubs, and other organizations. They serve on boards, they give their time and effort to various projects, they solicit donations of money. As soon as they lay aside one task, another is waiting. Some of them serve in numerous capacities at the same time.

To a degree this concentration of work and influence within a small group of able and willing leaders may be termed unavoidable. But it also tends to ignore the potential services of many persons who live outside the narrow limits of organized workers for the community. If enough of these were recruited to active service, in whatever capacity their background and skills would permit, it is conceivable that the rate of progress would be stepped up greatly.

The pattern of community work in most areas of the United States has been such that the leaders have come to assume that only a few persons, percentage-wise, are willing and able to take a hand in it. There is an alternative chance that many helpful hands have remained unused simply because, under the accepted routine, they were not invited to participate.

How to awaken their interest and set them in harness alongside those who are already at work on matters of common concern? There's the problem.

There, also, is a challenge. To the extent we find the methods for enlisting the interest and help of larger and larger numbers of citizens, to that extent we develop the resourcefulness of the community to meet its problems and move on to better living.

There is a sense of accomplishment and gratification

in contributing services which benefit the whole community. To assume that this feeling, or the desire for
it, is present only in a small percentage of people is
to manifest a degree of smugness not commonly attrib-
utable to the American people. The more reasonable
assumption is that the talent, skill, and experience of
many citizens are available for community improvement—as soon as we can establish the pattern within
which they can work.

II. Examples of Obtaining Wider Participation

1. Suppose a certain area is badly in need of a playground. It needs the services not only of money-raisers
but of artists, artisans, laborers, nurserymen, caretakers,
etc., etc. If the various responsibilities of construction,
maintenance, and operation are shared among many,
the burden in each case will be light—and will be
proudly borne.

2. Tree planting is a pressing need in many areas.
If a community undertook such a program, it could
bring into a co-operative effort almost an entire population. Children in schools could be set to studying various aspects of the problem. Area organizations of
residents could be formed to discuss and plan opera-
tions. Experts could be used to coach groups of volunteer workers. Committees could be assigned to care
for the trees after planting.

Out of such accomplishments might grow permanent
localized organizations for further activity. At the
least, a much larger group of people would have been
brought into the circle of community effort. The only
way to develop a sense of responsibility is by assigning,

or sharing, responsibility.   Through working together people learn how to work together again.

3. Almost any community can produce music and take pleasure in doing so.   This is a field where participants can be drawn from all levels.

It seems unnecessary to multiply examples.   In each case special needs mean special opportunities.

III. *The Advantages of Wider Participation*

1. More manpower at work on problems of common interest.

2. A more widespread feeling of belonging to the community and sharing its responsibilities.   The pride which comes with this feeling is infectious.

3. More channels of communication between individuals and between groups. Communication of ideas and voluntary sharing of work is the essence of democracy.

4. The enlargement of possibilities for community improvement.   Projects which could never be accomplished by 10 per cent of the people might be undertaken with confidence if 40 per cent had learned how to work together.

GUIDEPOST
17   *How to Plan a Meeting*

ALL OF US attend meetings.   Some we leave with a feeling that everything went off without a hitch; others, no matter how good the speaker may

Guidepost 17 by Irwin T. Sanders.

be, keep us squirming in our seats all evening. The little things that go to make a smooth meeting are so often overlooked that those having the responsibility of planning a meeting will do well to remember these points.

I. Working Up a Good Attendance

1. *Notify members.* Be sure that members are correctly notified of hour, date, and place. Allow plenty of time if notices are mailed; rely on the local newspaper only if most members are subscribers and if the paper will arrive sufficiently in advance of the meeting date. Ask some members to telephone, if possible, those who may not have received notices or who may not have attended last time. Tell members enough about the program so that they will know what to expect and will look forward to the meeting with anticipation.

2. *Irregular attendants.* Ask persons who have been irregular in attendance to take some part in the arrangements for or conduct of the meeting. Don't place too much of the planning, however, in unreliable hands.

3. *Transportation.* Ask the members with automobiles to go by for those who have no convenient way of getting to the meeting. Many people are quite willing to do this but never think about picking others up until it is too late. Quite often for important community-wide meetings school buses can be made available.

II. The Meeting Place

1. *Location.* Keep it central, if possible. If the customary location is not central, then hold the meetings from time to time in different parts of the community.

In this way, transportation hardships will not fall upon the same people over and over.

2. *Physical arrangements.* If a public building is to be used, check up several hours in advance on such matters as the key, heating arrangements, lighting, and custodial care. Find out who is responsible for putting the place back in order after the meeting and whether any custodian will be on hand to get what is needed just before or during the meeting. Discuss any financial arrangements relative to place of meeting before rather than after the meeting. If a private home is to be used, then find out whether the hostess would like any assistance in getting ready for the meeting. Will she need any folding chairs to accommodate the number expected? Be sure that all the physical properties necessary for the program are on hand ahead of time. Carefully check over the list of things needed.

3. *Adapted to size of group.* Choose a place that will suit the size of the group. Twenty people feel lost in an auditorium; on the other hand, if the room is too small, people are uncomfortable.

4. *Must be socially acceptable.* Be careful about using a place that is identified in people's minds with some organization of which they generally disapprove. Your group may have quite different purposes but will be frowned upon if it meets in a disreputable place. Remember that ideas about what is disreputable vary considerably from community to community.

III. *Preparation of the Program*

1. *Plan in advance.* Plan the programs several months in advance whenever this is possible.

2. *Assign parts to several people.* Have specific parts

of a particular program assigned to different persons. Be sure they have whatever helps they need to work up their parts.

3. *Outside speaker.* If there is to be an outside speaker, check with him about transportation to and from the meeting. If the engagement was made quite far in advance, a note reminding the speaker of the date, place, and time a few days before the meeting will often avoid a slip-up. Tell him about the program, so that he will know how much time he has and how to make his remarks fit the occasion. Careful planning will eliminate many last minute hitches, which so often turn what would have been a good meeting into a mediocre one.

GUIDEPOST
18

*How to Conduct
a Committee Meeting*

THE SUGGESTIONS for organization meetings and those concerning committee meetings in general give us a basis for some specific points on how to conduct a committee meeting.

1. *Committees differ, but procedure is about the same.* Committees differ in size from one to several members. Some are standing committees, and some are named for specific assignments. General procedure in meeting is about the same, however, for an executive committee composed of officers of the organization and for a special committee from the general membership.

2. *Chairman should not do all the work.* One mis-

Guidepost 18 by Howard W. Beers, Head, Department of Sociology, University of Kentucky.

taken idea is widely held. It is that the chairman of the committee should do all the work. A chairman can nourish or kill that idea by his leadership in committee meetings.

3. *A committee should meet for a specific purpose,* to accomplish part or all of the task for which it was named. A date should be set, and members should be informed well in advance of the date. Be sure that every member clearly understands that he belongs to a committee and that he knows the committee assignment. Each member should be asked to be ready with suggestions. Sometimes it is a good idea to ask each member to think about some special phase of the committee job, perhaps even bringing special materials to the meeting.

4. *Meet in a suitable place.* It should be free from distractions, noise, discomfort, or competing events. The corner of a big room in which a lot of other activities are buzzing is not a good place for a committee meeting.

5. *Have a proper emotional tone.* If you are a chairman, set the emotional tone of the meeting by opening with a combination of formality and informal good nature. Let it be known by your manner that the committee meeting is for business but that the business is to be accomplished in an atmosphere of good will.

6. *Begin promptly,* and announce that you expect to close the meeting at some set time. This will speed action and discourage dawdling.

7. If chairman, *guide or lead the discussion,* but do not manage or control it. Don't let your committee members become a rubber stamp.

8. *Prepare an agenda in advance.* If the committee has a secretary, he should help prepare the agenda.

9. *Start the meeting with routine matters:* minutes of the last meeting, reports of subcommittees, or members with special assignments, disposition of unfinished business held over from previous meetings, and finally disposition of new business.

10. *Get all members to take part.* Recognize and use each contribution of every member. Have all members express themselves on each issue or proposition. Keep the discussion on the track. Keep working for agreement.

11. *A committee meeting should be conducted by the chairman.* If a higher ranking officer of the organization is present, he must not take the committee chairman's prerogatives away from him. The report should satisfy the organization's need in the field represented by the committee assignment. One or two members of a committee can draft a preliminary report from their understanding of the agreement among the members. This report can then be modified or approved by the entire committee.

12. *If another meeting is needed, set a time for it before adjournment.* Assign specific tasks to each committee member in preparation for the next meeting.

13. *Accomplish something definite.* If the committee has a complicated assignment, restrict the work of each meeting to some phase of that assignment. Be sure members leave feeling that they have accomplished something.

19 *How to Preside at a Meeting*

PARLIAMENTARY LAW is a means, not an end. Its purpose is to facilitate orderly procedure. Parliamentary law is the outgrowth of centuries of human experience in the formation and operation of organized bodies. It is not sacred in itself but the most convenient method of doing group business.

I. A Few Simple Rules to Be Remembered

1. A motion is a formal proposal for group action made by a member and upon receiving a second generally takes precedence over everything else until disposed of or the group adjourns.

2. Nominations require no second.

3. The presiding officer is an impersonal, impartial individual who does not participate in debate except in special circumstances. His main purpose is to inform and aid in orderly procedure. He speaks of himself in the third person and is addressed impersonally.

4. In case of doubt over procedure, the will of the majority always prevails.

5. Speed may be obtained by avoiding unnecessary votes. Instead the chairman states that "Without objection it is so ordered." This is never to be employed on a controversial issue.

6. A motion may be amended, but amendments to amendments are bad, leading to digression away from the principal motion before the group.

Guidepost 19 by J. B. Shannon, Professor of Political Science, University of Kentucky.

7. A motion to table another motion must be seconded and put to vote. The motion that is tabled cannot be considered again at the same meeting.

8. Only a person who votes with the prevailing side may move reconsideration of an action taken by the body. Anyone may second it.

9. The previous question, when adopted, means that the majority has made up its mind to act and wishes no further discussion.

II. Four Basic Principles

Simply stated, there are four primary aspects of parliamentary procedure:

1. Democracy—the will of the majority comes before everything else and always prevails.

2. Fairness—liberty for everyone to be heard is offered, the majority willing.

3. Speed—one thing at a time and only one.

4. Courtesy—one person obtains the floor and nobody else speaks until he yields it or his time expires.

GUIDEPOST
20　　　　　　　*How to Prepare Publicity*

ORGANIZATIONS SHOULD keep their work before the eyes of the community by reporting their activities in the local newspapers and on the local radio stations. This is desirable not only for the vitality of an organization but also for the social development of the community as a whole.

Guidepost 20 by Pauline S. Taylor, Social Science Analyst, Bureau of Agricultural Economics. Information on radio furnished by Carl R. Taylor.

I. Why Organizations Should Report Their Activities

1. *Maintains status.* An organization which sees that its activities are publicized maintains and improves its status in the community. Giving out frequent information not only keeps its name before the community, but also tends to increase its membership.

2. *Keeps in the public mind.* By keeping the community informed of its activities it lays the groundwork for any community-wide program or campaign that it may foster. The community will only accept and sponsor those activities which it understands and in which it believes.

3. *Serves as incentive to members.* The members of an organization are more active and enthusiastic if they are associated with an up-and-coming group whose worth-while role is recognized and acknowledged in the community. Certainly, adequate news stories about meetings tend to increase membership as well as attendance at meetings. Too, individual efforts of a member of an organization which are noted and recognized in the local press and radio spur that person toward greater activity in his role as a member of the organization.

To be a social force in the community, then, an organization must keep before the community an accurate and up-to-date record of its activities and must stimulate the community to recognize the organization's awareness of and responsibility toward local problems.

II. How to Report Activities

Since it is to the advantage of each organization operating in the community to keep the public informed of its activities, the organization has the responsibility of seeing that the local papers and radio stations are fully and accurately informed of its meetings and activities. This should include notices that the meetings are being held as well as reports of the meetings themselves.

1. *Organizational reporter.* Each organization should have its own reporter whose duty is to write up accounts of all activities of the organization for the local newspaper and radio station.

2. *Announcement of meeting.* A brief announcement (75 to 100 words) of an approaching meeting should be turned in to the local paper and radio station several days before the meeting. This should include the time, place, date, and principal business or speakers. The newspaper will generally carry this announcement as a news item at least once free of charge. Since most local radio stations broadcast a social calendar of coming meetings and events at least once a day, they will include such announcements of meetings on this broadcast free of charge and often will make the announcement several times over a period of two or three days preceding the meeting.

3. *Report of the meeting.* The report should be accurate and to the point. It should be a clear-cut account of the who, when, where, what, how, and why of the activity or meeting being reported. That is, it should tell when and where the meeting was held; what, how, and why the group planned or carried out the program it did; who was present and who had any special responsibility for the meeting; and, finally, what plans were made for carrying forward the organization's activities.

4. *Names.* The account should carry *the list of names of those present* and those functioning in any special capacity. The reporter should be careful that every name is spelled correctly and that no name is omitted from the list. For radio it will be helpful to give the phonetic spelling of any names that are difficult to pronounce.

5. *Length.* The write-up should run from 250 to 500 words in length, depending upon what the organization has to report to the community. If it had an outstanding speaker at its meeting or if it plans to launch a program in the community, these things should be emphasized. The community wants to know what an organization is doing and planning, and the reporter should make his write-up long enough to inform the community of these things.

6. *Promptness.* The reporter should write up the account of the meeting as soon as possible after it is held. He should find out from the newspaper editor what time the account must be in and have it in on time. The radio station will want to use these reports on its local news broadcasts *as soon as possible* after the meeting is over. In cases of important speeches, advance copies should be secured and made available to press and radio so that they can have their stories written and ready for use immediately after the meeting.

7. *Getting report to editor.* If it is impossible or inconvenient for the reporter to take his account directly to the newspaper office and radio station, he may telephone or mail it. In the case of the newspaper, however, he must always keep in mind the editor's deadline, and in the case of radio, he must remember that the

newscaster would prefer a brief report immediately to a lengthy one twenty-four hours later. In either case, delivery in person at once is much preferred to mail or telephone reports.

III. A Word About the Editor

The reporter as a matter of policy should keep in close touch with the editor of the local newspaper and the news editor of the radio station, develop their friendship, and seek their advice and co-operation in reporting the activities of his organization. In this way the editors will be more aware of the organization as such and are likely to see that its write-ups are used in the newspaper and on the radio. If the occasion warrants it and he is properly informed, the newspaper editor may use the work of the organization or a specific program that it may be launching as the basis for an editorial, since he is always on the outlook for activities or programs in the community that make for pertinent editorial reading. The radio station may donate fifteen minutes of the station's time for a discussion of the program or project by the organization's own members. In such cases, the station's program director will assist in preparing scripts for the broadcast.

If the editors are not aware of the organization's activities and campaigns, however, they will overlook their editorial possibilities. In this case, the community, the newspaper, the radio station, and most of all, the organization will suffer because of the organization's failure to keep its work before the public through the local press and radio.

TOPICAL INDEX